Linda Horton's other books:

From Hell to Hallelujah!
Everyday Blessings and Miracles
Fear Not
Only Believe
Time & Again
Time Will Tell

Thank you to the wonderful Everman people who contributed information!

My Heartfelt thanks to my friend Linda Drinning Van Briggle who contributed the most in the gathering of information in order to get this book written. Linda spent time making phone calls to find Everman residents, old photos, etc. She reminded me of certain incidents, and encouraged me to keep going when in the beginning it didn't look as if anybody but she and I were interested.

Thanks also to Barbara Stockton Ross, Debra Ann Franks, George Gragsone, Jr., Gaylle Gragson Gregory, Johnny Ragsdale.

I apologize for any misspelled names, wrong dates, etc. I did my best to verify everything but I'm sure there are a few mistakes.

If you are interested in making contact with Everman Drive Residents, renewing old friendships, sharing wonderful memories of Everman, Linfield or Wilmer Hutchins, OR talking about the book, **Everman Drive***, go to* **Facebook** *and type in* **Everman Drive** *in the search bar.*
I'd love to hear from you!

Dear Cousin: Debra Ann Franks   2012
Looking back on the days of our Youth!

The Sun was shinning, Our Friends were Laughing
and we were Smiling.

We were blessed to be Loved by two Wonderful Mothers
on a Street we call! " Home " Everman Dr.

What a place , What Memories, What Character's
and you know if you look back on the Name
"Ever Man" that it was! a Place for Every...Man to live
The Rich , The Poor, The Young,The Old,
The Good and the Bad.
Every Man was welcome and was called Friend.

This was even the place we were saved and
 met the Lord .   Grateful !   So Grateful!
The Lord has been so good to us all, we could not ask
for more!

It was all' in his Great Plan for so many People to
cross paths in such a small Place called HOME
            " Everman Dr "
                         Author: George E. Gragsone Jr

INTRODUCTION

Charles Dickens in 1859 began his historical novel with the words: "It was the best of times; it was the worst of times . . ."

When I hear or see that classic line I, of course, immediately think of, *A Tale of Two Cities*.

But it also reminds me of another time and place in my own lifetime one hundred years later . . .

That place was **Everman Drive** in the late 1950's and early '60's; a half dozen or so residential blocks in South East Dallas, Texas. You'll hear that same sentiment from many, if not all, the people who lived there—as a matter of fact, I've included some thoughts and stories from several of them.

Why was it the best of times?

To begin with that time in our country was, in just about every way, a much kinder gentler nation. People weren't so angry, self-centered, rude, and mean!

Home and family:

People knew and helped their neighbors. They lived by the Golden Rule. Nobody ever thought about locking their doors—there was no need.

Kids, on non-school days, would take off in the mornings to hang out with friends, and wouldn't come home until the street lights came on in the evening. Neither the kids nor the parents ever had a thought of any kind of danger.

Clothes:

We actually wore clothes that covered our bodies!

Music:

Rock and Roll, the greatest music of all time, had just been birthed! We had Bill Hailey and the Comets, Elvis Presley, Jerry Lee Lewis, and Fats Domino. We learned the Bop and the Stroll by watching Dick Clark's American Bandstand on T. V.

Cars:

Those of us who were old enough to drive (or could hitch a ride with a friend who did) had the greatest cars ever: the '57 Chevy and Thunderbird, '58 and '59 Impala, the Corvette Stingray, the Lincoln Continental, the Chevy 409 with four on the floor! They were beautiful and we loved to show them off anywhere groups of teens could gather.

Entertainment:

We had drive-in movies, and Saturday matinees that cost twenty-five cents for those under twelve. Theaters offered two complete films plus a half hour or so of cartoons—which by the way were also wholesome, harmless, and fun; like Sylvester and Tweedy Bird, Tom and Jerry, Wiley Coyote, Porky Pig, and so many more. The drive-in theaters provided swings, see saws, monkey bars, etc. up under the big screen where the kids played before the movies and during intermissions.

Television was only a few years old, and the movies as well as the T. V. offerings were wholesome, family oriented productions.

We played cowboys and Indians on mop or broomstick "horses" based on the western movies where the good guys always wore white hats and the bad guys ALWAYS lost. A huge part of our cowboy costumes was holsters with "guns" that made popping sounds via Caps.

We idolized the Mouseketeers on the Mickey Mouse Club.

We hung out at local drive-ins where carhops skated or walked out to take your food orders and then deliver them to your car. (The Sonic and similar drive inns of today can't come anywhere NEAR the fun and experiences we shared at the original drive inns with carhops! More often than not, we'd pull into the drive-in, go from car to car socializing and just stay there until they closed. If you parked in the front row you COULDN'T leave until closing time because you were blocked in by two or three rows of cars behind you!)

Or, we circled the court house square or drove up and down Main Street at an extremely slow speed until midnight or later so we could see, greet, and/or flirt with all our friends and meet new ones. We called that draggin' Main.

Toys:

We, if lucky—and my brothers and I weren't—had bicycles, roller skates with keys that locked them on to your shoes, hula hoops, monopoly, checkers and Chinese checkers, Frisbees, BB guns, Lincoln Logs, tiny plastic army soldiers, Pick Up sticks, Jacks, Slinkys, Teddy Bears, Tinker Toys, Yo Yo's.

But the BIG ONE was: Barbie dolls that came out 1959. I wanted one of those dolls so badly! Mama had just married Menard when they arrived in my hometown of Greenville, Texas. I remember all of us going into a store and seeing the first one. The price was either $3.95 or $4.95. I pleaded for one but

Mama said we couldn't afford it, maybe I could ask for one for Christmas. I did, and hoped and prayed but never got one.

We never heard the words "electronic devices or games"! They hadn't yet been invented and I'm NOT SORRY to say I'm GLAD! My generation experienced a MUCH BETTER childhood hanging out and socializing together in the great outdoors!

Language:

People didn't use curse words as fillers in their sentences. They especially didn't curse or tell nasty jokes in front of women and children.

Business:

Sales clerks were ALWAYS polite to customers—even to "looky-loo's" because those "I'm just lookin'" people could be future customers. It was very rare that customers were rude or mean to clerks! The rule of business was "the customer is ALWAYS right!"

The Worst of times:

My parents were the most selfish, self-centered, damaged people I've ever met. It wasn't entirely their fault—they were both raised by extremely abusive parents. My father didn't have what it takes to realize and do something about his short comings, but my mother did and refused to even try. As a result, I and my siblings, suffered terribly; so much so that a couple of them were never able to overcome it. How any of us made it out of early childhood I don't know!

My Family:

I now believe my mother was bipolar but she was never diagnosed. She refused any attempt to get help or treatment. I believe she realized something was wrong but either didn't care or, couldn't stand the thought of it being verified by professionals. Growing up her home life was horrific. She was the second child and the first girl, out of twelve brothers and sisters. Her parents were horribly ignorant and abusive in just about every way one can imagine.

My first half-sister, Karen suffered serious learning disabilities and emotional problems all her life. By age twelve she had begun having extreme night terrors where she'd scream in the most blood curdling way never waking up and wouldn't remember it in the mornings. This went on for quite a while. Mama took her twice to a psychiatrist—NOT just a counselor or psychologist--but the top psychiatric doctor at Fresno County Hospital—paid for by welfare. The two visits consisted of both Mama and Karen participating in the sessions.

At the end of the second meeting the Doctor said Mama needed counseling along with Karen. Mama blew up, telling him he was crazy, the problem wasn't hers it was her daughter's! She refused to even consider taking Karen back for help. She railed for days to me and other relatives "How DARE that QUACK suggest I have a problem!"

I asked timidly if she might go and just pretend in order to help Karen. She blew up at me and screamed that I should mind my own business—she wasn't going to have some book-learning IDIOT who didn't know a thing about her, blame her for things that she had no control over! As a result Karen has suffered her entire life from huge problems, some of which might have been lessoned if Mama hadn't been so afraid of being told she was doing something wrong!

I got the same response from her when I was in my forties. Because we all had such problems—some more than others—I begged Mama to participate in group counseling sessions with all six of us children and I'd pay for them. She flatly refused! She stated she wasn't going to allow us to gang up on her and claim that everything was her fault!

I explained that wouldn't happen; the counselor would act as a mediator and he/she wouldn't let any of us just beat up on her. She wasn't interested. She said whatever problems we had we could just get over them! Unfortunately, my younger brothers and sisters didn't know how. I'm convinced that's what killed two of them! I did learn, but it took time and a lot of hard work.

I am the oldest of Mama's six kids. I think she may have been a little more attentive to me when I was born and little, but I don't ever remember her spending time with me, never hugged and loved me up, never did much talking to me, and always expected me to be perfect and grown-up. I didn't experience the kind of neglect and abuse my younger siblings had to endure! Yet I developed my own problems that I had to find a way to overcome.

From the time we were born mine and my brothers' lives were hard—our parents were damaged by their parents. But when our parents separated and divorced they both completely abandoned any type of parental relationship. They seemed to live for nothing but themselves and revenge on each other. Mama never missed an opportunity to tell us everything that was wrong in our lives was our father's fault.

Though we didn't see him often, and not at all after Mama hijacked us to California, Daddy badmouthed her every time he got the chance. But that wasn't anything unusual. He did that from the earliest time I can remember.

He'd tell me when he went to town or somewhere, "Linda, watch your damned ol' Mama and if any men come by you let me know when I get back, okay? Make sure she don't go up in the barn hay-loft with a man!"

I can remember that as young as four. As little as I was, I felt CREEPY when my daddy said stuff like that! Did my mother deserve it? I don't know. I never saw her do anything with anybody. Later, I gained information that caused me to wonder.

Could Daddy have driven her to it? Absolutely! He was extremely verbally abusive to her! Or maybe she did something and he caught her which caused him to become so mean. Both options are possible. In either case, they were like two cars crashing into each other at a hundred miles an hour, and we kids were the broken pieces of metal and glass that were strewed all over the sides of the road! The resulting "debris" was me, my two brothers: Frankie, four years younger, and Gary, six years younger, by my father Edgar.

After we moved to Everman Drive in 1959 Mama had a girl; Karen, and a boy, Terry Lee, by her second husband, Menard, whom she'd only known one month before marrying. Two years after we arrived in California she had a little girl; April, from a short affair with a married man. Because of Mama's choices and actions our lives got harder and the three little ones suffered even more!

Mama and Menard were newly married when we moved to Everman Drive. Menard had no idea how normal people lived and had no use for us kids. My mother did know better but her main goal in life was to have a man—any man! She'd do anything to get and keep one! It didn't matter who or what they were.

From her divorce from my father until she got so old she couldn't attract anyone, she frantically searched and moved into her home, any man that would give her a second glance. She was married at least five times and shacked up with at least eight or nine others for varying lengths of time. And that's not counting the ones she "dated" a time or two.

All of them except Menard were alcoholics. All except two had an aversion to work and were ne'er-do- wells that she supported with her California welfare checks which were supposed to be used on her six children. She bought their beer, cigarettes, food, clothes, helped pay their bills, and even helped to buy a couple of new cars, etc. She gave birth to six children but then expected them to raise themselves—we were all ignored, neglected and emotionally abused. My younger siblings were even physically abused by Mama's mentally ill parents and the different live-ins while she pretended not to notice. But no matter what she did to keep a man, none of them lasted very long; usually a couple to three months, once, only two days.

My father was even worse off. He was diagnosed with severe mental/emotional problems after a lengthy stay in a Veteran's Hospital mental ward when the army evacuated him from the Philippines. I discovered after I was grown he had to be put on Thora zine (an extremely strong psychiatric drug used to treat schizophrenia, manic depression, and severe behavioral problems). He also underwent shock treatments during that hospitalization. But as soon as he got some distance from the doctors he refused to take any medications. Even later in life when he developed diabetes and heart problems—the doctors would give him pills, he'd take them a few days, say he was well and didn't need them, and would throw them away. Part of his problem was he was paranoid about everything and everyone.

He thought doctors only wanted you to take medicine because it put more money in their pockets.

He was hospitalized for several months a second time for mental problems when I was seven. But some of his problems stemmed, at least according to him, from his abusive, angry mother, Bertie. He said she'd hated him and whipped him many times with a belt until blood ran down his legs. He claimed she didn't do that to any of the other three children. Because of his mother's treatment I believe he subconsciously hated women. Oh, he loved to flirt with all women, young or old, but when they didn't live up to his expectations—and no one ever could because it was impossible—he called them "heifers", "bitches", and worse. Even me, his only daughter, after I reached the age of about nine or ten and began to exhibit a mind of my own— which started when I told the Divorce Court Judge that I wanted to live with my mother.

My brothers and I were sent to visit Daddy once in a while after the divorce and he would often leave us with his parents while he went on a date or, to a café to sit and flirt with a waitress. It was obvious at a young age that he really didn't care much about seeing us. Mama would make sure she told us that over and over. Daddy refused from the get-go of the separation/divorce to pay even a dollar a month for child support because he was afraid my mother would somehow get a benefit from it. I must add though his disability income was so small he couldn't have given us much.

My Grandparents:

My father's parents, Bill and Bertie, hated my mother and didn't like us because of Mama—yet Grandma doted on her other grandkids. It wasn't so much my grandfather—he tried to joke around with us when Grandma wasn't looking, but he had to go along with her in everything she said or his life wouldn't have just been miserable—as it had to be with that bitter, selfish woman. It would have been impossible! Grandma ruled the roost!

Our maternal grandparents, Paw Paw and Mama Davis were mean, mentally ill, and abusive as well! After Everman Drive, Mama devised a devious plan to move us to California and in with her parents. We discovered what they were immediately after stepping off the train and meeting them. We never knew what to expect from any of these people—Paw Paw loved using his razor strap on his children and grandchildren until he was way up into old age. His punishment to one four year old great-grandson in the 1980's was to lock him in the trunk of a car on a very hot summer day and refuse to allow anyone to get him out for about twenty minutes. My mother was there and witnessed it along with a couple of her sisters and they did absolutely nothing! We had to walk softly and stay out of their way as often as possible.

But not long after Mama moved us to Everman Drive my life changed dramatically. That neighborhood was like a bright, shining light on a hill that guided me up out of a lonely valley of darkness. And it would influence me for the rest of my life. Mama jerked us out of there after only two years but I loved that place and those people. Unfortunately, I wouldn't realize how monumentally important they were until it was way too late. Our lives would only get harder.

That old saying, "You don't miss the water 'till your well runs dry" certainly rings true in the case of Everman Drive.

Chapter One

Everman Drive was a blue-collar neighborhood just off the Central Expressway, in the south-eastern part of Dallas, Texas. I was introduced to it in the late 1950's. A stranger passing through wouldn't have thought much of it. The houses were mostly small and old. There were empty lots here and there, and many of the houses were in need of a good coat of paint. But the yards were clean and mowed, some with—some without flower beds. The streets were kept clean of litter, and the neighbors were mostly friendly to each other—heck, a lot of them were related in one way or the other.

The people who lived in those houses were hard workers, several of them were house movers, some (including my stepfather, Menard) worked for the Dallas Sanitation Department, picking up garbage via the big city trucks. Others were auto repair mechanics, store keepers, restaurant workers, truck drivers, and housewives.

The elementary school was Linfield, the junior and senior high was Wilmer Hutchins. I don't know the history of the Everman Drive neighborhood. I lived there a relatively short time but those wonderful, good-hearted people helped me to develop and eventually put into practice my life principles. I miss it and over the years have thought of the people often.

While writing this book and talking about it with friends of my same age, several said, "Oh yeah, the neighborhoods were all like that back then!"

But that's just not true! They were NOT all like that. How can I say that with such confidence? Because my mother moved us an average of four times a year for many years starting with her divorce from my father, not only in Texas but California as well. Not one neighborhood, even in the same community—we lived in three or four different houses just four or five blocks away from Everman, and five different houses in the same neighborhood in California as well as other parts of town. Not ONE was EVER anywhere close to Everman! Not the adults or the children.

Everman was one of a kind. And it was all because the people who lived there were honest, kind, and caring. They weren't perfect but they lived by the golden rule: "Do unto others as you would have them do unto you." And they taught their children to live the same.

My initial introduction to Everman was not pleasant. I was eleven years old but had been through, and seen more, in my short years than a lot of adults. I felt old but was not yet cynical. I still had hope that things would get better.

My parents had divorced a year earlier and I'd had to step up in front of a Judge, my parents, paternal grandparents, aunts, and uncles, to declare who I wanted to live with. Mama had one person on her side of the court; her younger sister Margie. My mother's parents and brothers and sisters had all moved to California in 1950. Margie had moved back shortly before the court hearing and was living with us.

It wasn't easy for me to get up there. I didn't want to choose. No matter what I said somebody was going to be angry with me. I can still remember my father and his family glaring at me with somber, threatening facial expressions as I entered the witness box beside the Judge. The in-laws hated my mother, always had, and the feeling was mutual. Daddy hated her for daring to leave him even though he treated her like he hated her when they were together. They were all sending a silent message that if I chose my mother I was basically "dead" to them.

I loved both of my parents even though they were both hugely flawed. I wouldn't realize until later in life just how damaged they were. I grew up knowing the best thing I could do was be silent and stay out of their way. If I did that—and I always did my best-- I lived a somewhat peaceful life. If I didn't, I'd be screamed at, threatened, whipped, shamed or punished by silent treatment and mournful looks that telegraphed just how disappointed in me they were. But they were all we had and I didn't want to lose either parent or my extended family.

For several days before court I struggled as to who I would, and should, choose. I was choosing not only for myself but for my two little brothers as well. I wanted to make the best choice for all. In the end, the main reason I chose my mother was because at least she'd try to provide us with the basic necessities. Daddy didn't believe there was any such thing as a necessity. He lived on a partial monthly military disability check. He'd been "shell-shocked" in the Philippines and was extremely paranoid about everybody and everything. He'd only held one job for two weeks in my entire life. The only thing he ever voluntarily spent money for was land and the "left-over" livestock at the sale barn that nobody else wanted—that way he'd get them cheap. He had to be forced and shamed by his family members into even spending money on a doctor when we were extremely ill! That was partly because he was a penny-pinching miser but also because he hated doctors, possibly stemming from his "treatment" in the V. A. hospital.

Daddy's grocery list his entire life consisted of cold cereal, spam, Vienna Wieners, potted meat, canned pork and beans, peanut butter, and coffee. He saw no reason we should need anything different. He thought buying any kind of fruit was a waste of money and he didn't have much use for vegetables. At least Mama cooked red beans and potatoes every once in a while!

Plus, it never occurred to Daddy that we needed new clothes or shoes. He believed that you wore what you had till it absolutely fell off of you. He didn't think about baths, didn't ever ask if we had a toothbrush, or if we used one. Mama wasn't very attentive either but when we got to stinking she'd heat up water and pour it into the old galvanized tub for us.

So, at the divorce and child custody hearing I chose Mama, and paid for it for the rest of my childhood; more from Daddy's parents and sister Ruby, but he'd also make snide comments like, "Well now, how're you likin' living with your damned ol' Mama? Are you proud you chose that ol' heifer (which was his favorite nickname for her as far back as I could remember)?"

One thing I'll give my mother, she was always a hard worker, bringing in whatever money she could by picking soy beans and chopping and picking cotton every season. I remember vividly when I was six she got up two days after giving birth to my second brother Gary and began harvesting soy beans all day long, and the days after 'til the field was bare, while Daddy moaned and groaned and laid around the house complaining about not feeling good.

But Mama had her own mental/emotional problems as well. She was one of twelve kids but only seven survived babyhood. Her parents were extremely uneducated, strict fundamentalists, obsessed with sex, and verbally, as well as physically, abusive.

Paw Paw was very quick to use a razor strap (used in barber shops to sharpen razors) to whip his seven kids until blood flowed. And, he apparently didn't care how old they were when he started whipping them! Margie, one of Mama's sisters, at about age ten, witnessed Paw Paw take his three month old baby, Rebecca, out of a church service and "spank" her because she wouldn't stop crying. Margie says the Preacher and some of the parishioners witnessed it and "they came down on him hard" with him admitting he'd "made a mistake"! Mama was the second oldest and first girl, which meant she was responsible for the younger ones.

But though Mama was a hard worker, as I got older I began to suspect that she worked so long and hard for another reason as well: she liked work much better than taking care of her kids! When she wasn't working, she kept her head buried in *True Romance* magazines. She was never a loving, cuddly, playful person. After her and Daddy's separation, she became more aloof and would only get worse as time went on. We kids got attention only when something was wrong and even then only the attention that was absolutely necessary.

She was not a homemaker. She'd been raised in a filthy home and that's how she kept hers. She wouldn't cook very often so we went hungry a lot —her usual modus operandi was to, once in a while, bring home after work, a loaf of sliced white bread, a roll of baloney (she very rarely bothered to buy mayonnaise or mustard or anything to lubricate the bread) and maybe, if we were lucky, a block of cheese. My two younger brothers and I would eat as many dry sandwiches as we could hold because we were always hungry and never knew when we'd get more food.

I was left as young as age eight except when school was in session, to watch and care for my brothers while Mama worked, sometimes from sun-up to sun-down. My father wouldn't watch them—they made him "too nervous", so he made himself scarce around the home, piddling here and there but never doing chores, repairs, or any kind of work. To be fair, he did receive that partial disability check from his short military service in the Philippines. And, I discovered in my mid-thirties that he probably suffered not only from some sort of military injury but probably severe panic-anxiety syndrome, and/or agoraphobia, which I believe his father, my grandfather, Bill, also suffered from. Neither was ever diagnosed—not even the medical community knew or recognized anything about panic anxiety until about the early eighties.

Daddy also suffered from extreme lazy-ness. He had quit school in the eighth grade, never read a newspaper or listened to the news. But the main thing was he flat didn't like hot, hard work, and couldn't do anything else, even if he'd wanted to!

When I was in school and unavailable for babysitting my little brothers would sit under the cotton trailer or under shade trees at the edge of the soy bean fields all day while Mama chopped cotton, pulled cotton bolls, or picked the beans. She'd take a minute to check on them each time she finished her row. When Daddy drove her to the fields, which is the only way she could get there—she didn't learn to drive until her thirties—he'd play at picking up a hoe or a cotton sack for a few minutes but soon he'd start breathing hard, moaning and groaning, and would end up lying under the shade as well—as far from the boys as possible. If the boys needed anything, Daddy would rise up and call Mama. In his entire life (he died in 1997) the one job he held for two weeks was when I was about four years old. He worked for a dairy picking up and delivering those big old metal cans of milk. I remember that because he took me with him a time or two and I loved it. He never tried to work again.

Half the time Mama and Daddy didn't even know where we kids were or what we were doing! One time when I was about eight we'd spent all day out in the cotton field. Mama worked like a cotton picking machine, Daddy rested in the shade drinking iced sweet tea (until the ice finally melted) out of mason jars that Mama had packed for the day. I was taking turns watching my brothers and working a few rows of cotton—I was overjoyed when I could earn even one dollar.

At the end of the day we loaded into the car and took off for home. Half way there (we'd driven about five miles) Mama turned around and asked why baby Gary (who was about a year old) was being so quiet. I realized at the same instant that Gary wasn't in the back seat with us.

"Linda! Where's the baby?" she yelled as she turned around and jumped up on her knees in the car seat to search the back floor board. I jerked up and looked on the other side of Frankie but the seat was empty.

"Oh my Lord!" she moaned. "We left him in the field. Why didn't you say something, Linda?"

I had no answer, but saw quickly that it was turned around to be my fault. Daddy whipped the car around and went back to get him. He was still lying under the trailer, all alone, with a couple of cotton pickers still out in the field at the other end of the rows. Why I, (my oldest brother Frankie was only four) didn't notice Gary wasn't in the back seat with us, I don't know. I do remember that that scared me though. If Mama and Daddy could forget and leave the baby in the cotton field how could I be sure they wouldn't forget me someday?

I'm sure Mama was tired after work. I can't describe how hot, and energy-draining cotton picking was and we did it every season up to the divorce. Mama plodded along at a pace that others tried but could never keep up. She was very well-thought of by certain cotton growers in the Hunt County, Texas area for being able to pick 800 clean pounds of cotton a day (no dirt or rocks slipped into the sack to make it weigh heavier). Each hundred pounds earned her a dollar. Eight dollars a day was huge for our family, since the only other income was Daddy's disability check. Daddy was just too "nervous" to work but he had no problem with Mama working.

Yet with all this neglect and ambiguous attitude toward her children I remember at about age nine hearing Mama brag to someone, "I've taught Linda right from wrong, so I don't worry about her."

I remember thinking **HUH?! She didn't teach me OR my brothers anything!** She rarely even talked to us unless it was to scold or shame us!

Neither of my parents had any friends. We never had company over, not even family! Before I started school the only time I was exposed to others was once or twice a month on Saturday when we made a trip into Greenville for whatever supplies we might be able to afford. That was for me, a huge treat! We'd park at Market Square where there was a second hand store run by a man named Bob, who carried used comic books. I'd sit there and look at them (before I learned to read) and read them after I gained that skill, and wait until the Saturday matinee started at The Texan or The Rita Movie Theater. The theater ticket for me only cost a quarter and I'd be there from about ten to two or three in the afternoon. When it was time to head home we'd stop by father's parents for a few minutes, which didn't excite my mother. Once a year, either Thanksgiving or Christmas Eve, we'd go to a holiday dinner at my mother's Aunt Vera and Uncle Jesse's in Sulphur Springs. Later when I was seven Mormon Missionaries started coming around our isolated home to disciple Mama into the flock—Daddy wouldn't have anything to do with them.

We kids were always left on our own! I was so bored and lonely throughout my childhood. I ABSOLUTELY HATED summer and Christmas school vacations! And going to school observing the teachers, the other kids and the parents who volunteered as room mothers, etc., is how I knew at an early age that my parents, my whole family, were different from other people. I tried very hard to learn from those people how to act.

Once in a while I got to spend the night with my best friend Cheryl who lived with her little brother, Ralphie, with her grandparents, and theirs' was a whole different world. Cheryl's grandparents loved those two little kids and did whatever they could to show them that. They had a warm, comfortable, but no-where-near-fancy home, home-cooked meals they shared together at the table three times a day and a positive atmosphere. Of course, Cheryl may have felt different about it because the reason she and her little brother lived with their grandparents, I was told, was because her mother had been institutionalized (why or what kind? I never knew). Their father apparently felt he couldn't take care of them. Now, I realize there had to be a lot of sadness there but none of them ever showed it. When I stayed the night, the grandparents treated me just like they did their grandchildren.

Up until my mother finally left my father we were living in a big, old, unpainted house in Kingston, a small community located halfway between Greenville and Celeste. My father had purchased that house a year or so before. It still amazes me that although he never worked and only received that small disability check he could somehow afford to buy properties here and there. He was a tight-wad for sure and heaven knows he never bought anything for Mama or us kids, but he'd owned a thirty-acre plot a few miles from the Wright Cemetery, outside of Greenville and he'd bought an old house in downtown Greenville that his parents lived in for a couple of years. When he sold the town one, he bought a tiny, run-down little house with a couple of acres at the end of O'Neil Street as you leave Greenville proper.

After their separation my mother moved us into the house on O'Neal. Daddy stayed in Kingston. From that time until shortly after the divorce court proceeding, when we stayed with our father on weekends he usually deposited us at his parents' and disappeared doing whatever it was that kept him occupied. Grandma had always been a children-should-be-seen-and-not-heard advocate and she'd always let me know in different ways she thought I was too much like Mama. After court she was thoroughly disgusted with me. Granddaddy never said anything, he knew better than to cross his wife!

One of the things that we always knew to stay away from was Grandma's refrigerator. We were always hungry but weren't allowed to have anything other than what Grandma grudgingly put out on the table for us. It was usually left over "salmon patties" (made with canned mackerel from breakfast (which I admit I loved and still do!) or fried potatoes and cold biscuits. Now, admittedly Grandma and Granddaddy were poor. Granddaddy mowed lawns five or six days a week up into his old age so they didn't have much. But Grandma was so stingy. She always had cake, a pie, or a couple of donuts, and two or three Coca Cola's in her fridge. I remember asking her a couple of times if I could have some of her cake or sodas, and the answers were always a quick "No! That's for mine and Ruby's (her fat teenage daughter) "diet"! Granddaddy even knew better than to ask for any of the treats!

When Mama and Daddy separated Mama got her very first job outside of field work. She went to work at the local Dairy Queen. Now, in addition to rolls of baloney she would occasionally bring home hamburgers, left-over French fries or anything else nobody wanted. One of her younger sisters, Margie, who had moved to California with her parents and other siblings in 1950, moved back to Greenville and in with us on O'Neal. Margie was nineteen, eleven years younger than Mama. Margie immediately, upon arrival, went to work in a boat manufacturing company but complained about the fiber glass and didn't stay there more than a couple of weeks. She then got a job as a waitress in a café in town.

In the meantime, Mama met a customer at the Dairy Queen, by the name of Bud Abbot, and fell immediately "in love". He took her out once or twice. She even brought him home to meet Margie and us kids. He seemed nice and, to me, movie-star handsome. I had never met anyone like him and was impressed that my Mama could find somebody like that. But, after the first couple of dates, we didn't see him again and Mama moped around with red-swollen eyes and drooped shoulders for several weeks. She even took me to the Dairy Queen one day and had me try to talk to him. She wanted me, at nine years old, to find out and tell her why he'd dumped her?! I tried but he and I both were embarrassed and he wouldn't say anything other than he thought Mama was a nice lady and we kids were cute. She told me later she thought it was because Bud didn't want to be saddled with us kids—boy, nothing like having more guilt poured on you for your parents' unhappiness!

Daddy wouldn't accept that Mama was actually going to go through with the divorce and he probably heard she was dating. There were a couple of times before the divorce was final that he came by our house in the middle of the night and thought he was going to make some headway with her. The second time in particular scared me silly! I was sound asleep as were my two brothers. Margie was working a late shift. Daddy apparently snuck around to the window in Mama's room, quietly removed the screen, opened the window, and began to climb inside.

Mama started screaming, "Linda, Linda! Help! Call the cops!"

I jumped out of bed, ran to her door, and saw my father ahold of her arm trying to either pull himself inside or drag her outside. I didn't know which.

I heard him growl, "You old bitch! You ain't gettin' away from me!"

Well, I didn't know what he was trying to do. Was he going to beat her up? Kill her? What?! We didn't have a telephone. We couldn't afford one. We barely had enough for occasional food. I had to run in a panic next door, wake up the neighbors, and call the police. I don't remember what happened after that, except that I shook for a long time. But that would only be the beginning of the times I'd be awakened in the middle of the night by Mama screaming for me to call the cops when she took in some idiot who got physical. That can really take a toll on a kid's nervous system!

EVERMAN DRIVE

That time with Daddy I just remember the next morning overhearing Mama telling Margie that the cops weren't going to help her because Daddy had friends in the police department. That confused me; I'd never known Daddy to have any friends. How could he have them in the Police Department?

After Bud dumped her Mama didn't wait for her divorce to become final to hunt for another man. That would become a pattern. She wasn't a bad looking woman! She was only, at that time, about thirty, 5'8" tall and slender, had dark brown hair and eyes with olive complexion. The only thing that detracted from her appearance was that she'd had to have several of her top front teeth pulled several years earlier and because my father was so cheap she'd had to have the two front ones replaced with gold plating (she would get complete upper dentures in a few years). But her parents had spent all her growing up years telling their kids how worthless they were. My father spent the nine or ten years of their marriage reinforcing that, so I'm sure it was more than her looks that caused her to chase any man that would look at her twice.

Anyway, Margie came home from work one day telling Mama about this "long, tall, drink-a-water", named Menard, that kept coming into the restaurant with his brother R. C. who was also single, and asking her for a date. Margie was actually making fun of Menard. She told Mama he seemed nice but he wasn't the cleanest guy she'd ever met. He was also definitely uneducated and seemed to make up nonsensical words to express himself—things like "discompopulated" meaning nothing or nobody there, and "unconswerving" meaning someone wouldn't change his/her mind. He came up with non-words easily so it was obvious he'd grown up in a family that spoke like that.

But the most startling thing was he didn't seem to have ever been taught to use a toothbrush. Margie couldn't see herself getting interested in him. She sat around with Mama, making jokes about his breath and how awful it would be to kiss him.

Mama laughed right along with her and made comments like, "Wonder why nobody's ever talked to him about it?"

Margie replied, "I don't know, but could you imagine being romantic with him like that?"

Well, within just days, Mama found a way to visit Margie while on duty at the restaurant, at the right time that Menard and R.C. usually came in. Within a couple of days she had a date with Menard. She brought him home to introduce him.

I was horrified. The first thing I noticed, of course, was his teeth which were not just yellow, but closer to an orange color with cement-looking gunk stuck between them that even as young as I was, could tell it had been solidifying there for years! And, if you got within a couple of feet of him, you could smell him!

I couldn't understand why my mother would have anything to do with him! I kept remembering what she'd pounded into my head for years—although it had never applied to our house—that no matter how poor we were, we could always make sure our bodies were clean! And now she was fawning all over this ugly man who didn't know how to converse properly AND, didn't ever brush his teeth!!

It turned my stomach to look at his mouth but it was one of those things—sort of like driving by a bad car wreck that you don't want to look at but you can't keep yourself from it! It didn't seem to bother Menard at all. He'd open his mouth wide to laugh. Maybe he didn't know any better, I don't know, but you'd think a grown man (he was in his early thirties), no matter how uneducated, would have learned basic things like brushing his teeth early on.

I was horrified and confused. I mentioned to Mama how I felt about it about a week after I met him. She was very harsh with me, which was her constant response if anyone ever questioned anything she did or said. She said, "He can't help it that he didn't get to go to school and I can teach him to use a toothbrush. You should be ashamed of yourself! You're not Miss Perfect either, you know!" (Accusing me of trying to pretend to be perfect was one of her favorite shaming methods.)

One month after she met Menard, as soon as her divorce from my father was final, she announced that they were getting married the next week on New Year's Day. I was devastated! It was obvious Menard didn't like me or my brothers and we didn't like him. I was absolutely ashamed and disappointed that she would even date him—he was a dirty, smelly creep!

But they went through with it. Margie, me, and my two little brothers were her witnesses. They had a Justice of the Peace conduct the quick ceremony somewhere in downtown Greenville. Some jokes were made about an old wives' tale that said "whatever you're doing on New Years' Day you'll be doing all year long". I didn't see anything funny about that but the adults seemed to think it was hilarious. We all went straight back to our house on O'Neal. I noticed when we walked in the front door that someone had nailed a blanket up over the doorway that went from the front room into the bedroom that went off to the right, but I didn't think much about it.

We all sat around for about fifteen minutes, we kids not saying anything, Mama, Menard and Margie making small talk. It was New Years' day but it was three o'clock in the afternoon and bright daylight. Soon, I noticed Mama and Menard had disappeared. I still didn't think anything about it.

We'd never done it before but I wondered if we were going to do some sort of New Year's celebration that evening because of their wedding. I jumped up to look for Mama to ask her. I threw back the blanket over the bedroom door and rushed in to look for her. What I found was Menard, naked as a baby jay bird, on top of Mama in the bed going at it. It shocked the heck out of me! They both turned to look at me and stopped all movement. I was horrified and more embarrassed than I'd ever be again in my life!

OH MY GOODNESS!

I knew nothing about sex at that time except what I'd heard whispered at school but I sure knew what they were doing. It disgusted me and it still does today! They couldn't even wait until nighttime when we were all asleep?! To think they, in the middle of the afternoon, had to get it on right then with three kids under eleven, and a nineteen year old on the other side of a skimpy, worn blanket! Sickening!

I shot back into the living room as fast as I could, crying uncontrollably out of embarrassment and shock. Margie tried to comfort me but I wouldn't talk to her and ran into the back part of the house. I guess Mama and Menard finished up their roll in the hay, because we didn't see them for a little while. At that age I doubt if I could have even known how to define the word respect... but I lost even more of whatever it was for my mother that day!

After a few days life fell into a kind of new routine. Mama did get Menard to start brushing his teeth and taking fairly frequent baths. He didn't have a job so he hung around at home doing absolutely nothing but taking an occasional nap while Mama worked. He claimed he was looking for a job but it sure didn't seem like he was trying very hard. Mostly, he just tried to boss me and my brothers around. Frankie and Gary didn't like him either. Mama had never paid much attention to us but now she devoted ALL her time at home to Menard. And she'd told the three of us in the beginning: "If you want to, you can call Menard Daddy."

HUH?! *No way would that happen!*

Again, I was insulted and horrified but stayed silent which was the safest thing to do. Why would I call that freak daddy?! Although my real Daddy was far from perfect, had let us down many times, and even shamed us for staying loyal to our mother, we had a Daddy, and we still loved him! Frankie and Gary wouldn't call Menard Daddy either. (She'd try in the future to get us to call every man she moved in Daddy as well—we always refused!)

About three or four weeks after the wedding ceremony, Margie moved into her own apartment. By then she'd become interested and started dating one of her male restaurant customers named Bill. He seemed nice but he was an awful lot older than Margie—he had to be at least in his late thirties or early forties, but she seemed quite comfortable with him. Not too much time passed before Margie and Bill married and moved to Fort Worth.

That left me and my brothers alone a lot with Menard. We tried our best to stay away from him. He had nothing to say to us UNLESS he was angry. Did he try to get to know us? I don't think so. We simply weren't important. I don't think he was evil. I just think he was ignorant. He'd never been married before, or had kids and only heaven knows what his family was like. Who knows if he'd even dated before Mama—with those filthy teeth who else would have agreed to date him? The bottom line was, we just didn't matter to him—and not much to Mama—she spent all her free time hanging out with him in their room, and left us to find whatever we could to occupy our time.

The next three months were a strange time for us kids and it's mostly a blur for me. Daddy and his parents were mad at us for not turning against Mama. Margie was busy with her new boyfriend, and Mama and Menard were too busy with each other to notice us. I was in the fourth grade at Travis Elementary School so I had some diversion. My two brothers weren't old enough yet for school. Frankie was going on six (there was no kindergarten) and Gary was four. They stayed home with Menard while Mama continued her employment at The Dairy Queen. Menard started in right away trying to be a "father" to the boys by ordering them around, whipping them when they didn't do what he said, and ignoring them the rest of the time. The boys hated him.

The one incident I remember during that time happened on a day I was at school. Even though it could have been a horrific tragedy I admit I, at my young age, thought it was pretty funny, and just what Menard deserved—although I absolutely never had any wish that he be injured or worse! I just wanted him to be GONE!

We never had the money to pay for garbage pick-up. We had to deposit our garbage on the small covered back porch in a big old thirty-gallon, rusted out, metal barrel and sooner or later somebody would haul it off for us. On this day, as usual, the barrel was stuffed full of a little bit of everything; food scraps, cans, papers, cardboard—who knows what else? That afternoon the boys were running around trying to find things to do and Menard was laid up in the bed taking his daily nap. I don't know why the boys grabbed the matches. Maybe, they were trying to help get rid of the garbage? Or, maybe they were just curious and wanted to see what would happen?

As far as I know, they had never before or after, played with matches. But they found them, took them out to the back porch, lit one or more, and flung them into the barrel.

About the same time that Frankie yelled, "Let's get outa here, Gary!" and they started running to the back of the lot, Menard appeared at the back door and saw the flames eating at the porch ceiling. He grabbed the water hose and put the fire out. The underside of the porch roof would always have the blackened boards but it could have been so much worse.

What woke Menard up? He didn't know, but it was a good thing because the boys didn't even think about him. From that point on Menard decided naps might not be such a good idea while watching a six and a four year old.

We muddled on in that house, which belonged to Daddy, without paying any rent, until school was out. Which, of course, caused Daddy to be livid! Menard decided he would have more luck finding a job in Dallas. So, as soon as Mama could pack up a few clothes and spare necessities, we loaded up Menard's old station wagon and headed to the metropolitan area, leaving our dilapidated furniture and other belongings behind.

As we were driving along one of the Interstates outside of Fort Worth they spotted an old, empty house sitting right next door to a gas station, out in the middle of nowhere. They stopped and got the owner's name and information from the guy in the station. A few hours later we moved our scant belongings into that house and then Mama had Menard drive her to find a job, leaving us three kids alone until nightfall.

She was successful and went to work the next day in a department store soda fountain. Menard made himself scarce as well—he never came home until she did. The three of us kids were left in that hot, empty house, eight to ten hours a day, with nothing to do, no radio, TV, or telephone, and most of the time no food. Mama would bring us a small hamburger or bologna and white bread for sandwiches when she got off work. Somehow, Menard got a hold of a large card board box of individually wrapped caramel candies, and I remember being so hungry we'd eat on those until we finished them off.

We lived in that old house for a couple of months and then they moved us into a ram-shackle dump in a questionable neighborhood in Dallas. Mama had switched jobs to another cafeteria. Who knows what Menard was doing? We were living there when school started in September, but I didn't have any shoes so I couldn't register. Mama was informed by one of her co employees that she could get in trouble for keeping me out of school and that the local school district had some sort of charity fund where they'd buy kids shoes and certain other necessities if you applied and met the application requirements. She signed me up.

We did meet the requirements and I was embarrassed about having to accept charity, but was also excited. I was going to get a brand new pair of shoes, never worn before by ANYBODY! Daddy usually made us go to the second hand store for our stuff and since they'd been divorced we hadn't had the money to shop for anything, anywhere. I'd been LONGING for a pair of the very popular "Mary Jane's" that all the other girls were wearing. They were black and had a strap across the top of your foot. I thought they were so special.

Well, I showed up at school that first day barefoot and the social worker drove me immediately to a shoe store somewhere in that area. When we walked inside the first thing I spotted was a pair of the popular Mary Jane's. I squealed and pointed to them letting her know that's what I'd been dreaming of.

She shook her head and growled, "No, those won't last very long, we're going to get you a pair of Oxfords!"

My heart dropped! All the girls were wearing Mary Jane's. Oxfords had been out of style for a while and I hated them! I was almost in tears but held back. The school Rep. forced me into a pair of brown and white Oxfords, paid for them, and took me back to school wearing them. She didn't buy any socks so I really looked and felt stupid! This was the Bobby-socks era and for years I'd had to wear stretched out second hand bobby socks and put rubber bands on the tops to hold them up on my shins. But now I had no socks at all—every time we moved, Mama left the bulk of our belongings behind in the old houses.

I wanted to hide but had to wait until Mama came to get me. This was a Monday. I went to school the rest of the week wearing the oxfords, but by Friday Mama decided we were moving again. That Friday was the last day I ever wore those shoes. I don't know when or where I got a different pair or how, but I was glad to throw those things out. However, I was embarrassed and ashamed that my Mama had seemingly ripped off that school district. She didn't seem to give it a second thought.

We moved out of that district into another old house out in a rural area where we stayed for about a month. When we moved there I got excited about the possibility of joining the school band and learning to play the Sax, I hoped! The other schools I'd been to didn't have a band but this one did. I'd always loved music and was so excited. Well, I discovered when I got there the only band instrument left was a French horn. I was disappointed but tried it anyway. I practiced every evening but hated the sound of it. We moved again at the end of the month so I wasn't disappointed when I turned it in.

Chapter Two

Shortly after that Mama went to work on the early morning shift at Kemp's Café in the Everman Drive neighborhood. She moved us to another rural dump. She had to be at work at five a.m. so she made us kids wake up at four in the morning, get our clothes on, and climb into the back of Menard's battered station wagon where we'd go back to sleep on a ragged old quilt in the rear parking lot until time for me to get up and walk to school. By that time Menard had found a job as a helper on a garbage truck (at that time helper was the official title of the job per the Polk City Directories) for the City of Dallas.

Did my brothers have to stay in the car till Mama got off work? Probably. I know we did that routine for at least a couple weeks after I started school at Linfield Elementary which was in the Everman Drive district. My first day at school I learned a field trip to Proctor and Gamble had been scheduled for that Friday. I was excited. I don't remember going on a field trip with any of my prior schools, except a once a year play day at the big park in Greenville when I went to school in Celeste. But even though I was looking forward to the field trip I was a little nervous since I didn't yet know anyone.

To complicate matters on the morning of the trip I discovered while waiting in the station wagon for time to leave, that I was bleeding. Mama was inside the restaurant working. I had no idea what to do but was determined not to miss Proctor and Gamble!

For emergencies Mama kept a sack of extra clothes for the boys in the station wagon. I found an old, ratty but clean, white T shirt and folded it up to use as a napkin. I didn't mention it— I don't think I ever told anybody! I knew what was happening because my daddy's mother, Bertie had told me a little a few years earlier. I went on and participated in the field trip, checking for leaks the entire day.

Procter and Gamble was interesting. They showed us how they made soaps and other cleaning agents. Of course, anything different than the day to day routine in class was wonderful— not half as fun as the annual day trip to the park in Greenville but better than nothing. Plus, the P & G people sent home little sample sacks for our parents and gave us cookies and punch for a treat. Fortunately, that old T shirt got me safely through the entire day. I threw it away when I got home and snuck some of Mama's Kotex. I'm sure she eventually had to notice but again nothing was ever said.

It didn't take long to make a good friend at school. Linda Drinning and her brother Kenneth were both in my class and Linda and I became fast friends. By that time, Mama and Menard found a house to rent back a ways just off Everman Drive.

My friend Linda and her family lived a couple of blocks from us down Everman on the corner of Slagle in a big house they'd recently had moved in on the empty lot. There were several different families on Everman that made their living moving houses; the Cantrells, the Gragsons (who were related), and others. I later got to know many of them.

However, I did not know the people who lived in the little white house that sat directly behind our rental facing Everman. There was a well-worn foot path from the back of our house through the side yard of that house and I used it at least once a day, sometimes more, to visit my friend Linda.

The house itself was a cute little thing with matching garage, well taken care of—not anything like the different houses we had always lived in. It had a beautiful new white paint job with black trim. The yard and flower beds were well tended and there was a new looking chain link fence that ran down the side between that property's driveway and the one to the house next door. Since there was a well-worn trail from my back yard through that property to get out onto Everman, I just naturally thought that was the neighborhood short cut. So every time I left home to go to my friend Linda's I took that trail.

I didn't notice the first few times anybody in the house looking out at me but eventually it became obvious. She was a small, older woman with gray, sort-of bushy hair, staring out one of the windows with an ugly frown and glaring eyes. That old saying "if looks could kill" would come to mind. The more I saw her the more I wondered why she looked so mean. She reminded me of one of the witches in the fairy tale stories I'd heard, and movies I'd seen like *House on Haunted Hill* with Vincent Price. She was very thin, never wore any make-up, had that gray, witchy-looking long hair that stuck out in places, and she'd just stare out at me with that witchy, mean look, but never say anything.

After seeing her the first couple of times I made sure I walked as close to the chain link fence as I could get but she followed me with her eyes all the way out onto Everman. After a while she started coming out on her back steps to glare, hands on hips, but still never said a word.

I wondered what was wrong with her! I thought maybe she was crazy. Maybe she couldn't speak. I'd met someone like that a few years earlier. I'd even been introduced to an older blind lady who had asked me if it was okay if she touched my face with her hands. I'd said yes, but it felt weird and I'd been embarrassed. Mama told me later that was how some blind people figured out what people looked like. So, I just chalked this strange woman up to different strokes for different folks and kept walking through for the four or five months we lived in that back rental. I kept my eyes on her at all times because I didn't want to give her the chance to sneak up on me!

I couldn't stand to stay home, it was just too miserable! Nothing to do, nobody to talk to, nobody caring whether I came home or not, house filthy (always the norm), Mama and Menard gone, either at work or wherever.

When we left that back rental we moved into an old house behind Shepherd's Grocery store down at the end of Everman just before you got to Linfield Road. That's where I got to know Arlene Shepherd, another girl in my class. She was a very nice, somewhat quiet girl with long, brown hair that was always curled very prettily over her shoulders and back. She wasn't allowed to go anywhere in the neighborhood except school. She had a younger brother and both had to work in the store with their parents when they were home.

I really liked Arlene. A few times when I was home and bored I'd go into the store just to say hi and talk a few minutes but she always acted extremely nervous, eyes flicking around to look for her parents. She'd tell me she couldn't talk, that she'd get in trouble if her parents caught her. I asked her a couple of times to go with me to Linda's or somebody else' house to visit, but again she'd say she wasn't allowed to go outside in the neighborhood. That seemed so strange but I never found out why. Finally, I gave up and just spoke to her now and then at school.

Linda's family was exactly the opposite of mine. Linda had a fun-loving, cheerful mother, a family-loving father who wasn't home often because he was a truck driver, and seven brothers and sisters from, at that time, age 16 down to a fairly new-born brother. Their house was always clean and homey. Linda's mother loved kids and anybody her kids brought home was okay with her. I spent a lot of my time there and loved it.

Linda, her younger sister Nelda, and I, would pick up coke bottles off the side of the streets to turn in for; I think it was two pennies deposit. Or, we'd save up dimes and nickels we earned here and there for doing small chores for different people, and then would walk a heck of a long way over to a stable to ride horses for a dollar an hour. I fell in love there with a horse named Ace and would ask for—and usually got him every time. I didn't know until decades later that little Nelda also loved that horse and didn't appreciate that I "always got Ace". However, she never complained or argued about it, she only verbalized her frustration to her sister, Linda.

Once, Linda and Nelda were allowed to go with me and my little brothers to Greenville, about an hour away, to spend the weekend with my Daddy. Linda's mother never met my mother or my father but if she had she probably would not have let her daughters go. But it was a much gentler, trusting time back then—not so many mean or weird people, especially in the Everman neighborhood. Mrs. Drinning was such a good person; I don't think it would have ever occurred to her that anyone else could be negligent or strange. Thankfully, Daddy was on his best behavior that visit so we had a lot of fun. Mainly because he always had horses and we got to ride as much as we wanted—which kept us out of his hair as well. It was a good visit and Linda still remembered it vividly fifty something years later.

Linda was the only friend that I ever invited to spend the night because our house was always so dirty and disorganized. That happened when we lived in the house behind the "gray haired witch". Another reason I didn't invite people over was I never knew if my mother was going to be in one of her silent-crying, long-suffering martyr, or raging moods over something Menard said or did. She'd done that as long as I could remember, but with Daddy it had been mostly the silent treatment. She'd started the crying jags and silent depression with Bud Abbot, the short-term boyfriend before Menard in Greenville. Or maybe she'd always done them; I was just too young to remember. Now, she was pregnant with Menard's first child and continued to work in the restaurant as long as she could (back then a woman couldn't continue to work in jobs like that after she started noticeably showing). Later, Mama would graduate to screaming suicide threats: "I'm gonna stick my head in the oven!" It was just too embarrassing to think about anyone seeing the mess, and the fits Mama threw.

I did find out when I was seven and we drove to see my grandparents in California, where Mama had picked up her "housekeeping skills". She'd learned well from her mother! The only difference was Mama Davis did put meals on the table three times a day.

I'd even tried a few times before we moved to Dallas to make a difference in the disaster which was our house but gave up. What I was able to do didn't put a dent in the filth. I just made sure I never let any of my friends come inside or find out how we lived.

Linda did spend that one night and I think it went okay, but that was the last time I'd take that chance.

Many decades later, after I'd tracked Linda down and we'd renewed our friendship she mentioned several times how strong that memory of spending that night at my house was. I cringed when I heard that.

I thought *Oh no! She remembers our filthy house or my crazy mother or creepy stepfather!*

But no! What she remembered so vividly was that when my mother got off work and came home that night, she brought hamburgers for all of us. Linda remembers that burger as being one of the best in her entire life! She explained that with eight kids in her family they hardly ever got any kind of restaurant food. What she couldn't know was that we hardly ever got food, other than bologna and cheese—period! However, when someone made a mistake on food orders at the restaurant, Mama would get whatever it was if she could, and bring it home, which we would thankfully devour! Funny how two people in the same situation can remember two completely different experiences.

I did try one other thing at the same house though: I wanted so badly to have a party—I can't remember why—but knew I couldn't let people come inside. So, my friend Linda and I hooked up an extension cord through a side window, placed an old radio on a little table outside the window in a small grassy space between the house and the fence, and invited a few classmates over after school. It didn't occur to me that someone might have to use the bathroom—what would I have done then?

Well, I didn't have to worry about it, only one person besides Linda, Major Hammett, showed up. It was just as well, we had no refreshments, no games, nothing! Major went home and Linda and I found something else to occupy our time.

During most of our friendship, Linda and I just hung around her house. She was a homebody and didn't go out into the neighborhood a lot except for the horse stable when we could dig up the money. I just always wanted to be anywhere other than my home! Plus, Linda and I got along real well and no matter what we did we had fun.

My first year at Linfield Elementary had some good and some bad. I liked it okay with the exception of a couple of negatives: the first was two female classmates, who shall remain nameless, and their on-again, off-again, female "side-kick" (depending on how much the side-kick bowed and scraped to the two "leaders of the pack").

The main leader and the side-kick lived in a little "better" neighborhood over somewhere behind the school. The second leader lived in an RV in a trailer park in the other direction. From what I remember the one in the trailer park wasn't expecting to stay in our area very long. The three of them—I thought of them as hateful snobs—thought they were so much better than the rest of us. They did have better clothes than mine and Linda's. They constantly made fun of, or gossiped about us, and did everything they could to try to make us miserable.

But ever so often, the two leaders would get mad at the side-kick and boot her out of their "club" for two or three days. When that happened, she'd come running to us to whine and cry about the way they were treating her. The first couple of times we felt sorry for her and let her hang around with us. We'd sympathize and tell her to ignore the other two.

Then three days later the two leaders would forgive and take her back and she'd tattle any and everything we'd said to cheer her up which would make the leaders mad and cause them to launch a major cat-like assault against us. We finally learned our lesson. We realized we couldn't help the side-kick AND, she only wanted to use us as companions while the leaders were "punishing" her for whatever "disloyalty" they felt she'd committed! The side-kick was just as mean-hearted and even more two-faced than her leaders.

One day Linda finally got REALLY fed up with the side-kick. She can't remember if it was during the fifth or sixth grade. She and the side-kick were playing tether ball against each other with several other classmates standing in line waiting to take the place of the loser. All of a sudden Linda and the side-kick rushed each other and started punching. The side-kick grabbed Linda's hair and they went at it, eventually landing and rolling on the ground.

The Principal went running out and broke them up. Linda's face was blood red and her hair was wild. The side-kick had scratches and red spots on her face and arms. The Principal marched them straight to the office where they stayed for a considerable time. I didn't remember this incident. Linda told me about it while I was writing this book. I think it must have either happened in the sixth grade of which I can remember nothing, or it was on a day when I was absent. I'm positive I wouldn't have forgotten that. It would have been the first physical fight I would have witnessed. Plus, it involved my best friend who did not go looking for fights. And, it was caused by one of my and other classmates, "enemies".

I asked Linda: "Was it a real fist fight?"

"On my part it was!" she responded. "If I had to fight I didn't just pull hair!"

"Well, who won?" I asked.

Linda giggled and said, "I think the winner was the Principal. We both got in big trouble and then I probably got a spanking when I got home!"

The two mean-girl leaders especially loved to torment another classmate named Gaylle, who also lived on Everman Drive. I never knew why. Gaylle did have nicer and more clothes than Linda and I, but she never bothered anybody. She was our elementary school "champion" tether ball player. Nobody, not even the boys, could beat Gaylle at that game! She had the most powerful swing in BOTH hands and it took no time at all for her to wrap that ball around the pole leaving her opposition with their mouths hanging open and eyes wide!

That was just one thing that the leaders held against Gaylle. They were always trying to beat her at that game and just couldn't do it! Gaylle and I didn't hang around together much outside of school but I liked her and was one of the first, along with Linda, to go to her defense when the three mean girls started giving her a hard time.

Linda knew Gaylle a little better than I. Linda's brother Kenneth, who was also in our class, had a huge crush on Gaylle and vice versa. Linda and I couldn't help but let the constant harassment from the three female snobbish bullies bother us from time to time but we did the best we could to stay away from them.

Gaylle, on the other hand, didn't seem to let the episodes of meanness get to her. If nothing else, when she was being harassed she'd just go out alone and practice bashing that tetherball to kingdom come! Which seemed to irritate the mean girls even more.

My number two negative at Linfield was Math. In all the other subjects I excelled, especially, English and Writing. One of our teachers was Mrs. Stuart. I liked her a lot. It was in her class that I started making up and writing mysteries much like The Nancy Drew series. Mrs. Stuart read every one and encouraged me to keep it up. I had been an avid reader ever since I'd learned how but loved writing stories even more. It was also an escape from my home life. It was in her class that I decided I would someday write a book. About what, I didn't know. I just knew I had a book inside me somewhere! Mrs. Stuart told me I could absolutely reach my goal.

Another positive was a classmate named Daniel Ivy, who was only at Linfield a short time but made a huge impression on most, if not all, of us girls. He was a cutie and very nice. The song *Poison Ivy* was popular that year. We substituted the words Daniel Ivy for Poison Ivy and sang the song that way. We girls were "in love". Unfortunately, Daniel liked the mean girls' leader, which none of us understood. But oh well, that just gave us another reason—as if we needed another one—to dislike her! We were all very sad when Daniel moved away.

It's strange that I don't remember a single thing, not even the teacher in the sixth grade—our last year at Linfield. My friend Linda had to tell me as I was writing this book that the sixth grade teacher was the Principal and his name was Mr. Willis. She remembers there was a door from our classroom that led into the office and says that sometimes he'd have to slip into the office for a few minutes to take care of business. I can't picture him or anything that happened in that grade, at home, or at school. I think I've, for unknown reasons, blocked that year out. Something may have happened because there were always awful things going on at home. But it's perplexing because I remember vividly lots of activities and circumstances during my first through fifth grades—even most of the teachers' names and a lot of things from seventh grade on. But who knows? Year after year things at home got progressively worse.

In September of 1959, Mama had her baby, a little girl she named Karen. By that time we'd moved up and down Everman at least three more times. Two weeks after having Karen, Mama returned to waitressing at a run-down truck stop—I can't remember where it was or what it was called even though I went there several times.

I was eleven. My main goal in life was to hurry and get old enough to work so I could start buying pretty clothes. There was a nineteen year old, chubby girl—I can't remember her name—who worked at that same truck stop. She befriended me and when she was on duty would let me go behind the counter and do little things like fill water glasses, clean counters, bus tables, fill ketchup bottles, etc. Goodness knows I needed friends but she was also teaching me new skills that would help me someday get a job. She lived in a little cinder block storage shed that had been turned into a bedroom out behind the restaurant. Mama let me spend the night with her one night and I wised up quickly that there was something going on with that girl that a lot of people probably didn't know.

The beginning of the sleepover started out with silly girl talk, listening to music, experimenting with makeup, etc. She had to get up to open the restaurant early the next morning so we went to bed fairly early. About three in the morning someone started banging on the door and woke us up. It turned out to be some guy she knew. She went outside and talked to him a few minutes, then came back in and went back to bed. She said he was one of her friends. I got the feeling she may have had more than one "friend" who made late visits when the mood struck them. I didn't tell Mama but I never stayed another night with her.

Shortly after that, Mama quit that truck stop and rented a tiny little café—I think it was called "Mom and Pop's", on the Central Expressway just a few blocks from where we lived on Everman. It came with an old house out back where several elderly retired men lived. Part of the rental deal was that Mama would continue to feed these old men for free a couple of meals a day. Menard still worked for the sanitation department.

As soon as she rented the café, Mama moved us into a junky triplex down a little trail on the opposite side of Central Expressway from Everman Drive. By that time school was out for the summer and it was getting hot and humid, which is the norm for east Texas. The tiny apartment didn't have a cooler or even a fan, no telephone, TV, radio, nothing to keep me or my brothers occupied. Mama was to manage and operate the café and I, at eleven, was ordered to be the caretaker for my brothers, then seven and five, and little Karen who was about ten months old.

Mama and Menard got up at four every morning and were at the café by five to open and get him something to eat before he went to work. And by the way, he not only got a hot breakfast, she packed his lunch, AND, he was there for dinner and desert.

I was on duty with the kids for the same hours, seven days a week. Our food was cold cereal (often without milk because we had to save what we had for the baby until someone went to the store), bologna and wieners slapped between white bread slices, unless or until, there were leftovers from the restaurant that couldn't be saved and used the following day. We didn't get a lot of those because the old men that lived in the house out back had to be fed and they loved Mama's cooking. She was a very good cook—she cooked in the southern style with lots of butter, sauces, and sugar. She just wouldn't do it much unless she was at work, OR, she had a new man to impress. And remember everybody that ate free from the café was eating up profits which were scarce to begin with.

Mama was the café cook, dishwasher, waitress, janitor, everything. Menard did absolutely NOTHING but sit around in the café before and after work and gab with the old retired men or some of his work mates who came in once in a while. Even on weekends he'd sit there all day and listen to the jukebox. Mama had been given a key so she could operate it without having to put money in it.

Mama never said a word to Menard about helping out in the café or at home, or with the baby—until months after she had to close the restaurant down. I guess it never occurred to either of them that I, or my brothers deserved a break, or that his baby needed any parental attention!

One day about mid-summer I was given an un-asked for, un-expected, un-appreciated break in the mind-numbing routine Mama had forced on me. One of Menard's work buddies who was probably in his late twenties or early thirties and had an ex-wife and a couple of kids, snuck over to our triplex to see me while Menard was hanging out at the café. Menard allegedly had no inkling this was happening. I had seen this man a few times before but had never said more than a polite hello to him.

He apparently had developed a "crush" on me. I'll never forget it. I heard someone calling my name out front of the apartment and looked out a window to see that it was him. My brothers were out roaming the neighborhood. I was alone with the baby. All the windows and doors were open because of the heat. I couldn't imagine why this guy would be there. I answered him but wouldn't go outside. I could tell he was trying to flirt with me.

Even at eleven I was shocked and uncomfortable and knew something was way off. However, even though I felt uneasy, I did sit inside on the window sill a few minutes with the screen separating us and talked to him—mostly answered his questions—because one thing my parents had taught me was to be respectful to adults. I didn't know how to get rid of him. After a few minutes he finally left walking back in the direction of the café so he had to have left his car over there. I DID tell my mother about that. She told Menard to tell the guy how old I was and that he better not come around me again! He didn't. He didn't come back to the café either.

I was locked up in that hot, horrible dump of an apartment with a small baby seventeen or eighteen hours a day, while my brothers were out running wild in the neighborhood! There was, on the property, a tiny merry go round and a little waist-high bar the boys used sort of like monkey bars to do flips and as a pretend horse, but that got old and boring very quick! So, they ran all over the neighborhood doing who knows what all day long.

About the first week of August the boys had been playing on the merry-go-round and I happened to look out and see two Mexican girls a couple of years older and bigger than my oldest brother Frankie, beating him up. Two smaller girls were standing back yelling encouragement. Gary had stepped back a little ways somewhat in shock, too scared to move.

I ran out immediately yelling at the big girls that I was going to whip their butts if they didn't get the heck out of there. They all turned to run and I yelled after them they'd better not EVER touch my brothers again. I was very angry and in protective mode. Frankie was pretty shook up, the girls had given him a good what-for.

I took both boys into the apartment and tried to find out what was going on. I got nowhere. They both claimed they didn't know. I found out later when school started that Frankie had been bullying the two little girls and their bigger sisters were finally taking him to task for it. With no parental oversight and direction which none of us ever had, Frankie, in the next several years just got worse and worse. Gary never became a bully but he did develop lots of other problems. One of them was that Frankie bullied and picked on him all the time and made his life miserable.

That was absolutely the worst summer of my life! I admit I left the baby in the play pen just about all the time. I did feed her when it was time but I was so miserable in every way possible, I didn't play with her and I wasn't all that prompt at changing her diapers! I wasn't mean to her but couldn't help it; I did resent her and couldn't help but partially blame her for having to be a prisoner in such a horrible place. After all, if it wasn't for her I wouldn't be stuck in that hot filthy apartment day after day, hungry, miserable, lonely, and bored out of my head! I was a kid! I shouldn't have been forced into the position of raising a baby, especially under those circumstances!!

Why Mama wouldn't make Menard come home and watch the baby a little bit I couldn't understand. But, in the years to come I'd see that any man—and there were plenty that Mama drug home—wouldn't have to do a single thing—most of them didn't even have to work! If they wore pants and would give her a second look she'd take care of them for whatever time she could get them to hang around. Her kids . . . not so much!

Chapter Three

That same summer of my "imprisonment" one of Mama's sisters, Rosemary and her husband Jack, who lived in Central California popped in for an unannounced visit. Jack was a truck driver who made frequent runs into the South and Rosemary decided to come along with him on that trip. They pulled up and knocked on the triplex door. I'd been taking a nap. Baby Karen was asleep in the play pen. The boys were out wandering the neighborhood as usual. Rosemary and her husband came inside the filthy apartment, went to the play pen which was in the middle of the postage-stamp size living room and discovered Karen had had a bowel movement and it was all over her from head to toe. They were horrified and so was I!

Rosemary grabbed Karen and gave her a quick bath, put clean clothes on her and took her with them over to the café where Mama was working. I don't know what, if anything was said. When they finished their visit Rosemary brought the baby back to me. Mama never mentioned it. She didn't try to make any changes either.

I was stuck the rest of the summer in that crummy hot "box" while the baby's father, Menard sat on his lazy rear end, passing the time of day in the cooled restaurant until Mama finally realized she wasn't going to be able to make a go of it. She gave it up and locked the doors for the last time about the beginning of school in September. I turned twelve on September 2nd and Boy was I ready for school or anything other than being locked up inside a house! Once again we moved back over on Everman Drive.

My summer of "incarceration" had caused a breach in my friendship with Linda—I didn't see or talk to her that entire summer. We were again in the same class at Linfield in the sixth grade but as mentioned before even though I've ALWAYS had a great memory, I can't remember a single thing about that year! That is so weird. I can, believe it or not, even remember things that happened when I was as young as two and three years old! However, that entire year in the sixth grade is like a deep black hole in my memory. I can't even remember the three mean girls that year, though I know the leader was still there because she continued on during the seventh and eighth grades in different classes. Who knows or cares what happened to the other two?

Soon after we moved back to Everman I met the two girls, Charlene and Belva Stockton, who lived in that cute little white house with black trim where the gray-haired "witch" had stared out at me when I used the walking trail the prior year. The people who lived on the opposite side of the chain link fence that I clung to when I walked through were Charlene and Belva's cousins—another Stockton family who had several children. One of the youngest girls was Barbara, who I got to know and pal around with from time to time.

I remember going with Barbara a couple of times to her Grandma and Grandpa's house on Everman Court which was just down the street a short distance from her house. That little Court had three or four tiny houses on it and if I'm not mistaken both sets of Barbara's grandparents lived there. The Grandma we went to see, as I remember, (which might or might not be a true image) was short and stocky, had dark hair and a dark complexion. She scared the heck out of me! We only stopped by her house for a few minutes both times but I don't think her grandma ever said one word to me. She did stare at me the whole time without blinking, in what I thought was a mean, threatening look! After the second time I wouldn't go to her house again. While writing this book I was able, with help, to track down Barbara and as we were reminiscing I mentioned how scared I was of her grandma.

She laughed and said, "That had to be Grandma Stockton!"

She added, "I never understood that but several people have said the same thing to me over the years."

She went on to explain that she thought her Grandma Stockton was part Cherokee Indian and that's just how she looked. But, Barbara said she was the "sweetest thing" always slipping her some money!

All three Stockton girls, Barbara, Charlene and Belva, were very nice, friendly, fun girls. Barbara was a couple months older than me and had beautiful sunshine-blonde hair. Charlene and Belva had dark hair. I liked the three of them a lot but Charlene the older one, who was two or three years older than me became a close friend. Her sister, Belva, closer to my age, was very quiet and though I saw her often, we never really palled around.

I also got to meet the "witch" who turned out to be Charlene and Belva's mother, Ethel, and found out she wasn't a witch after all! She was really a nice woman. She treated me politely, although a little distantly. Her daughters explained that she had greatly resented that I had used their yard almost daily as a short cut to wherever I was going. That was my first clue that I had been doing anything wrong by following that footpath through their yard!

I wouldn't know until Linda told me, fifty years later, that that lot had been vacant for a long time before the Stockton's moved their house and garage on the property. So that foot path had probably been worn down years before they moved there.

As an added attraction Charlene and Belva had a very cute, fun, eighteen year old brother, William, called Willie by some. He had dark blonde hair, was soft spoken and almost always had a twinkle in his eyes and a smile on his face. Of course, I was just a little neighborhood girl so I didn't get much attention from him except he did like to good-naturedly tease me—about any and everything just because my face would flame red. I developed a huge crush on him but had no hope he'd ever notice me.

At the end of my sixth grade year it became obvious Mama was pregnant again. By that time Mama and Menard were having trouble. Mama was always in her silent, crying, "Oh woe is me, poor victim" mood. She spent a lot of time out in the back yard in the evenings after dark leaning against the house, moping — we were too poor for patio or garden furniture—heck we couldn't even afford the furniture we needed inside the house! Menard would be inside doing I don't know what. Many times I'd have to hunt Mama down to ask her something and I'd find her crying silently out in the dark backyard. She'd answer my question and that was the end of it. I don't know how long she'd stay out there. I was just glad to get away.

Just before my thirteenth birthday my memory returns almost in Technicolor like a movie on the big screen! Mama had just moved us into a house on Lackey Street which T'd into Everman Drive. That house was only a block from Linda's house but still I didn't see her. I don't know why. One of our new neighbors was Harry Lee and Mary Drinning, my friend

Linda's oldest brother—although I hadn't met either of them until Mama moved us next door.

I don't remember how I met Mary but we became friends very quickly. She was a cute, tiny little dark haired thing, always smiling and happy. She was sixteen years old and had a son, named Sidney, who was about a year old. She stayed home caring for the baby and the small house.

Her husband Harry Lee was eighteen, tall, strong, very confident, and good looking. He worked as a helper for the Dallas sanitation department. They had gotten married when Mary was fourteen and Harry Lee was sixteen. Somehow the three of us became close and I basically started living at their house, sleeping on their couch, eating with them, etc. I only went home when I needed a change of clothes.

Just before school started that year my brothers and I got a huge surprise. My father came by which he'd only done once before in the last two or more years and invited us to spend a week with him. That was extremely unusual! I wasn't sure I wanted to go. I was very comfortable and at home with Mary and Harry Lee but something made me change my mind and the three of us went with him.

By that visit Daddy was back in the big old, unpainted three bedroom house in Kingston where we'd all been living when he and Mama first separated. For a while he'd had Grandma and Granddaddy living with him but he'd never gotten along with Grandma so she and Granddaddy had gone back to a tiny house on Daddy's older brother Alvin's property. Before moving back to Kingston he had had a little two bedroom house moved onto his thirty acres out in the country behind the Wright Cemetery. That's where he was living when Linda and her sister Nelda had gone with me for the weekend. He'd lived there until one night while he was in town, a huge thunderstorm caused lightening to strike his television antennae and it caused a fire which didn't do a lot of damage to the structure, but did burn out the wiring.

    I think now, the only reason Daddy came for us that summer was that he was lonely in that big old Kingston house—but why I don't know. He'd seldom had time for us before. Even when he had made a few efforts in the beginning of the divorce he'd leave us with Grandma and Granddaddy—which always made me feel worthless. Can you imagine not seeing your father for months at a time and then when you did go to visit him, his "dating" or flirting with waitresses was much more important than spending those couple of days with you! The only weekend he ever seemed to try to "entertain" us was that weekend that Linda and her little sister Nelda had stayed with us.

    It quickly became obvious that visit that he might not be as lonely as I'd first thought. There was a married couple that had moved in next door to him that he'd apparently become friendly with. The husband worked long hours and the wife stayed home all day with their three year old daughter. Daddy was over there quite often talking to the woman, playing with the little girl, or he was talking about the woman—how nice she was, etc. I got the distinct impression something was going on! They just acted a lot more "friendly" than neighbors usually did AND especially between Daddy and his neighbors. He was ALWAYS (his entire life) something of a "hermit"! But it could very well have been that Daddy was flirting and TRYING to get something started.

    I liked her too. She was nice to us kids. She cooked a couple of good meals for us; talked to me like she cared, and made us all feel at home. When she found out my thirteenth birthday was coming up in a few days she offered to host a party at her house— volunteering to do everything. All I had to do was invite a few of my closest friends from Celeste and Kingston that I had gone through first through part of the fourth grade with. I had kept in touch with several of those kids and really missed them so I was excited. I'd NEVER had a birthday party before! My mother didn't even bother baking us a cake on our birthday. Sometimes she'd say happy birthday . . . IF she even remembered the date.

So I used the woman's phone and called four of my long-time Celeste friends. I'd been told I could invite eight people but I didn't have anybody else's numbers so I told the friends I called if they saw or talked on the phone to the other four to please invite them to my party as well. I gave the four the address in Kingston where the party would be and hung up so excited but a little worried. I did feel special but there was only three days until my party and I was afraid the other four kids wouldn't get the invitation in time.

I didn't have anything to wear to my party so at the woman's urging Daddy took me by a second hand store a couple of days before the party—he didn't believe in EVER wasting money on new clothes, but he was trying to play the "great Dad" for the woman. I found a cotton straight skirt I liked for fifty cents. I'd wanted a straight skirt for a couple of years but never had one. The only problem was it was way too long. Daddy said the woman would probably hem it for me if I asked her. He paid for it and we went home.

I'd never had any clothes that were popular! My time at Celeste was the era that girls wore the big circular skirts with several flouncy, puffy petticoats under them and they ALWAYS wore bobby socks! My socks came from the second hand store with the tops stretched out and not really fit to wear.

I'd only had maybe two or three new dresses in my entire life and those had been hand sewn by Mama out of print feed store sacks, which was fairly common in that day and age. And though the skirts to those dresses were gathered, they were BARELY GATHERED, not circular enough, nor long enough for petticoats anyway. So, though my party clothes wouldn't be anything my heart longed for, at least I was getting something, and it was something I'd wanted for a long time. I counted my blessings. The woman did hem my skirt and the day of my party when I was dressed and ready she pronounced me beautiful!

Early in the morning of the party the woman had decorated her little house with birthday things, baked a homemade double layer cake, made sure there were soft drinks, lots of ice (it's hot and muggy the first of September) did some last minute spiffing up of her house and then looked me over, did my hair, put a little blush on my cheeks and light pink lipstick on my lips.

Then the guests began arriving! And they kept coming, and coming and coming! All told there were about twenty kids, mostly boys that showed up. But my eight invitees all made it. The rest I had seen at school or on the bus except a couple who were apparently cousins or friends of the attendees. I don't even know if they all knew me. They could have just heard there was a party and headed over.

I, and the woman hosting my party, was shocked! She only had that one little cake and a couple of half gallons of ice cream and no time to put together anything else. I was embarrassed at first and promised the lady I'd had no idea so many people were coming—I hadn't invited them. All the kids that came were polite, good people. It turned out to be a wonderful, fun party so I got over the embarrassment very quickly. To make it even more exciting every one of the boys were cutie pies!! The few girls that were there, including me, were in teenage-girl-heaven.

After playing a few records and a few people dancing to songs like "Rockin' Robin", "Rock Around the Clock", "Hound

Dog" and "Jail House Rock" to my surprise the woman suggested we play spin the bottle and post office. Oh my goodness, I'd heard of spin the bottle but I'd never ever played it I'd never even heard of Post Office! I had to whisper to the woman that she'd have to explain what we were supposed to do. With a twinkle in her eyes and big smile she explained that in one, or maybe even both of the games, whomever was "It" got to take a little walk outside down the country lane and back with the "winner".

I took a bunch of short walks with different boys but even with spin the bottle, I did NOT kiss anybody! I was way too shy! And so were the boys. Here were boys—all of them a little older than me—several who I'd secretly thought of as "dreamboats" and they were paying so much attention to me that I thought I'd died and gone to heaven. Yet all I could do was take a short walk and smile at them! They grinned and blushed right back.

I don't remember how we survived the cake and ice cream fiasco with twenty or so kids but it didn't really matter. That was my first birthday party and I felt like a beautiful princess for weeks afterward. It was also the last time I ever saw all those Celeste kids.

I went back to Everman Drive a few days later and didn't get to go back to my Dad's:

A. because pretty soon I was working a full time job at night after going to school all day, AND,

B. because of a horrible trick my Mother would play on us a little later.

If I'd known that weekend of my thirteenth birthday party that I'd never spend any more time with my Daddy or Celeste friends I would have been horribly sad but as it was, I was glad to get back to Mary and Harry Lee's. I told Mary all about my party and basked in the after-glow of my "popularity" of that magic night—something I'd never experienced before. It felt good but it didn't last long. It couldn't make up for all the years I'd been ignored, neglected and put down by my parents and grandparents. Mary kept telling me that I was beautiful and lots of people liked me but I didn't believe her. However, I knew she did and I was grateful for that.

After school started I'd awaken every morning on their couch to the radio playing Floyd Cramer's *Last Date*—don't ask me how it happened to play at the exact time every morning. I loved that song and still do! It always makes me think of my months with Mary and Harry Lee and my crush on William Stockton.

Mary and Harry Lee would get up at the sound of the alarm, she'd make our breakfast, and Harry Lee would take off for work. Sometimes, Mary would work her makeup magic on me that made me feel so glamourous. Of all the people that I knew and loved in that neighborhood, those two were my all-time favorites.

They, even as young as they were, provided everything that was missing in my home. Harry Lee, at eighteen years old, supporting a wife and baby (and a little later a second baby), even paid for my food!! It never crossed my mind until I got much older that I might have been a financial burden to them! How many eighteen year old boys would not only support a wife and child but take on a neighborhood kid—no relation—and provide for him/her?

Harry Lee was one in a million!! They were both cheerful and positive; they gave me attention and advice in every matter, including boys. And Harry Lee even scolded me pretty harshly a few times when I did something unknowingly, that he thought was not proper for a young lady. That always broke my heart but I'd never do whatever it was again!

For instance, during that same summer there was some sort of celebration at the baseball stadium located on Linfield Road where Everman dead ended. It could have been Fourth of July but somehow I don't think so because I remember whatever it was happened during the day. It was hot but just about everybody in the neighborhood turned out (except for my mother and stepfather of course, who never ventured out to meet ANYBODY!)

We were all sitting in the stadium seating that was several rows high watching something. I was sitting with Charlene, her sister Belva, and their cousin Barbara along with some of the other neighborhood girls. William Stockton, the eighteen year old that I had a secret crush on and that loved teasing me to watch me blush, was sitting in the row right behind and above me with several of his friends sitting at his sides. Others were sitting all around us. Harry Lee and Mary were over a few seats above me to the other side with some of their Drinning relatives. After a while my back sort of cramped from not having anything to lean back against. I didn't even think about getting up and leaving! I was having too much fun. William moved his legs and said something to me and I innocently asked him if he minded if I leaned my back against his legs for a bit. He said no, so I leaned back and it really did help my back ache.

After a few minutes he apparently became uncomfortable and spread his legs out a little farther. I thought nothing about it—I was innocent—I hadn't even experienced my first kiss and definitely hadn't had anyone have any kind of birds and bees talk with me! I only knew the barest minimum about sex and that was only because I'd been raised on a farm with animals and heard whispers at school. When William repositioned I stayed where I was but I put one elbow up on each of his knees and kind of held my back straight by bracing my arms on his legs. I stayed like that a few minutes until he moved again. About then the get-to-gather ended. We all got up and went home.

When Harry Lee walked in the front door he stomped over to me furious. In a loud voice he said, "What do you think you were doing out there today?!"

I had had a great time and had no idea what he was talking about. He let me have it verbally! Finally, he had to explain what it was I'd done because I had no clue.

He said, "I'd better not EVER see you sitting like that again, between some guy's legs! What do you think everybody that saw you thought?"

I was shocked, embarrassed, and humiliated. I'd had no idea I was doing something that looked bad. I burst into tears and couldn't even answer him. Harry Lee was the protective big brother, a great all-American upstanding male influence that, whether I liked it or not, was looking out for me and my reputation. I learned a lot from both he and Mary and believe with all my heart that my life would have been a great deal harder if not for the love, friendship, and guidance they gave me! They were my greatest influence and just at the right time.

Harry Lee was angry for the rest of that evening but didn't say anything else. I was devastated. I'd embarrassed, disappointed and angered him and I was inconsolable. By the next day he was his old happy, fun-loving self again but I've never forgotten that day.

I don't want anyone to think I thought Harry Lee was perfect. He wasn't, and when I knew him, he never claimed to be. Neither was he a prude. He was a one hundred percent American man (even at eighteen years old) honest, hardworking, responsible, and he loved his wife.

One day when Mary and I were sitting around their tiny kitchen table talking, he came in from work, shed his jacket in the living room, walked into the kitchen, pulled Mary up out of her chair, gave her a big kiss and said, "Whoo Boy! I'm gonna ride that old bear tonight!"

Mary, stepped back, her face turned red, she gave him a playful slap and exclaimed in a shocked voice, "HARRY LEE!"

He just grinned, patted her on the rear and went on through to the bedroom to change clothes. I sat there silently with a blood-red face not knowing where to look or what to say.

Mary looked at me and said something like, "Sorry 'bout that. Don't pay any attention to him."

Then we changed the subject real quick.

Chapter Four

Mary enjoyed doing my hair and putting on and teaching me about make-up. She loaned me her clothes (which weren't fancy but much better than mine!) including a dark brown Mouton (fake fur) coat that she let me wear to school a few times that winter. My regular coat was a reddish brown plastic jacket I'd found at a second hand store for a dollar that looked like it had had a hot iron placed at the waist level pocket on the left front side. It was all melted and ugly but it was all I had. When I carried my books I'd carry them on that side to hide the burnt spot—this was before back packs. I tried to put up a tough front when I wore it but I was really embarrassed and insecure.

I entered the seventh grade at Wilmer Hutchins Junior/Senior High School right after my thirteenth birthday. Junior High was a whole different experience! I caught the bus at a little grocery store that was located on Everman Drive. It was owned by the Gilberts, an elderly couple who lived in the house next door to it. It was located directly across the street from Charlene Stockton's. They sold only the necessary items but had every kind of candy and soda that you could imagine. As often as I could afford it I bought a candy bar and an RC Cola before jumping on the bus in the mornings. Where I got the money I don't remember but the cola was six cents and the candy bar was only a nickel.

Having the little store as my bus stop caused me to get to know Charlene a lot better. I think she had quit school much earlier but I'd see her often, usually in the afternoons when I got off the bus. I'd hang out with her a little while and then head for Mary and Harry Lee's.

At Wilmer Hutchins every class was taught in a different room with different teachers but I only remember two. The worst one was an absolute nightmare! He was Mr. Henderson, the math teacher. He was horrific and got away with it. He may have contracted Polio in his early life because he had something of a deformed arm, hand, and leg on one side of his body—I'm not sure it was polio, just guessing, but polio was a big thing in the 1950's. I don't know if that caused him to be mean but something did! He LOVED scaring and embarrassing his students! And he certainly succeeded with me!

I've mentioned before that I began having problems about the fifth grade with Math and I continued to struggle but wasn't even close to failing, just having problems understanding the concept. However, Henderson made it much worse! He'd force five or six of us at a time, up to the blackboard to work out problems and if we made a mistake or couldn't finish the problem he'd throw a piece of chalk or an eraser at us and make fun!

We could be sitting in our desks and if we didn't answer just like he wanted, an eraser or piece of chalk would come zooming across the room and hit us, sending chalk all over our clothes, hair and everywhere else.

I was scared to death of him and hated that class. It caused my brain to freeze when he'd ask me a question, which of course, would cause me to get hit with something as well as a verbal tirade about how dumb I was.

He did this to everyone in the class that had a problem with math. And, he'd have a big grin on his face all the while. He was mean and everyone including the staff knew it. That affected me for the rest of my life regarding Math! When I finally made it to college I had to take a statistics class in order to graduate with my Bachelor's Degree. I ended up with an A in the class but it was a struggle every single assignment and I dreaded each and every class. After college I could do everything I needed to do with math but I still freeze when anything but the basics come in to play because of the abuse and humiliation I received from Mr. Henderson.

The second class was P. E. (Physical Education) with Miss Perry, a tiny, dark, pretty teacher who I'm sure had to be disgusted with us girls quite often. Up to seventh grade most of us had had two fifteen minute recesses and one half hour lunch break. At Celeste during first and second grade we'd play Red Rover, a little soft ball, or we'd play on the swings and seesaw. Beginning later in the second grade basketball became a huge thing—the Blue Devils have ALWAYS been big on sports and they took (and still take) a lot of pride in their "Lady Devils"!

Unfortunately, my parents took me out of Celeste for several months—right when they started our classes in basketball. We moved to Little Deer Valley, Arizona, to meet, live, and pick Pima cotton (which could grow as tall as the adults) alongside Mama's parents and siblings who trekked there from Central California for the same reason. We lived in a little temporary farm workers' community in a one room wooden "box" that had only a tie-down tarp for a roof. All the adults, everybody that is EXCEPT my father, picked cotton from sun up to sun down to make as much money as they could before the season was over and we had to all go back home. My daddy continued his

"Ohhhhhhh, I'm so sick I can't work . . ." *but I sure can flirt with all the pretty women pickers every time I get a chance*, attitude.

I and my mother's three youngest sisters and brother, Tina, Rebecca and James Henry, who were just one, two and three years older than me, went to school every day and picked whatever we could after school and on weekends. I have to admit my young aunts and uncles did have to work harder than me or they could get a "taste" of my grandfather's wrath and possibly the razor strap.

By the time I got back to Celeste my classmates were doing very well in basketball and I couldn't. I had never been taught or participated in—really never even *seen* sports games—and it just wasn't my "thing". I hated it, probably because I was so clumsy and couldn't seem to get the hang of it. The more I failed the more I dreaded it, and the more I made mistakes. I STILL don't care for and don't watch sports! Never have, never will . . . . (EXCEPT for professional bull riding—which shouldn't be too big of a surprise, I'm a true full-blooded TEXAN!)

While in grade school at Linfield in the Everman district we mostly did whatever we wanted, and that usually meant tether ball—which I never became accomplished at either. So, when we got to Miss Perry's P. E. class a lot of us didn't appreciate having to change into a one piece gym uniform and do the forced group calisthenics, running around the gym or track, jumping jacks, etc. The only way we could get out of participating was if we were "having cramps". So, a lot of us had cramps at least half to three fourths of the month, every month! When we'd tell Miss Perry that she'd look at us with a knowing look but she would excuse us and we'd go up and sit on the stadium seats, visit with each other, and watch the girls who actually liked getting all hot and sweaty.

Miss Perry was no dummy she knew we were faking! But back then things were much different. Women who were pregnant and working in the public had to quit when they began to show, and they might as well not waste their time applying for public jobs if they were pregnant and showing. When they gave birth they were kept in bed—sometimes in the hospital for a week or two. It was thought that exercise was a definite no-no for pregnant women and probably not good for females who were having their periods. Because of my negative attitude toward the ugly gym wear and sports, and later my tiredness from going to school all day and working eight hours every night, P. E. was my second least favorite class.

As mentioned before when we made it to Wilmer Hutchins and seventh grade, Linda and I saw each other infrequently. Neither did I have any contact with her brother Kenneth, nor Gaylle, or anyone else from Linfield except to see them from a distance at times in the hallways between classes. If it hadn't been for Mary and Harry Lee providing friendship and support while going through the problems with my screwed up family, and the problems with the violent math teacher I don't know what I would have done. Those two people, Mary and Harry Lee Drinning, teenagers themselves, were my rocks and my foundation.

As my seventh grade year marched on I became closer friends with Charlene Stockton and began spending a lot of my spare time with her. Mary was now pregnant with their second child, not feeling very well and busy with her toddler. I was still sleeping on their couch and very seldom saw my mother and family members, which was okay with me and apparently okay with them—no one ever came looking for me.

One night just after my thirteenth birthday as Mary and I were sitting around talking and Harry Lee was up at his parents', William Stockton came driving up and knocked on the door. I figured he was looking for Harry Lee but got the surprise of my life when he said, "No, I want to see you!"

He then asked if I wanted to go to a party with him. He told Mary it was a very tame get-to- gather over at George "Son" Gragson's house, and since it was a school night he'd have me back in a couple of hours.

The Gragson's were Gaylle's parents—my Linfield school tether ball champion/classmate. They lived on Everman a little closer to the end near Linfield Road.

I couldn't believe it! I'd had a crush on William for a long time and here he was asking me for a date. My very first EVER date!

"I have to go ask my mother," I told him.

"He smiled. "I'll wait."

I ran next door and frantically looked for Mama. It was dark so when I found the house silent and all the lights off I knew I'd find her moping out in the backyard. I could tell she'd been crying but I ignored it—that was a common occurrence. I just gushed out my request.

I was so excited I could barely speak.

"Mama! William's here and he wants me to go to a party with him! Can I please, please please?!"

All she said was "Who's William?"

"He's my friend Charlene's brother. He's very nice," I told her.

She said, "Yes, just don't be out too late."

I took off running back to Mary's.

Oh my gosh! My fairy tale dream was coming true!

When I got there Mary and William were sitting on the couch talking.

I burst in and said, "Yes I can go, but I need to change my clothes!"

William grinned and said, "Okay, I'll go and be back for you in fifteen minutes. Is that enough time?"

I was so excited I was shaking like a leaf. Mary jumped up and helped me change into one of her outfits and run a comb through my hair. She sprayed me with her perfume, dabbed some blush and lipstick on me and I was ready to go.

William was back on time and we left. I don't think we said a word during the three or four block drive to the Gragson's. William got out, opened the door for me and smiled, telling me I looked cute.

I was already super nervous but by the time we stepped inside the front door I was terrified. There were four or five adult couples sitting around the living room. I had no idea how to act or what to do but knew immediately I was out of my element—all those people were in their early to mid-thirties and I had nothing in common with them! I looked around for Gaylle. Neither she, nor her little sister, was present. William introduced me to all the adults—I had met several of them before including Mr. and Mrs. Gragson, but never really talked to them. They were PARENTS, for heaven's sakes!

Silly me asked where Gaylle was. Mrs. Gragson said the two girls were in their room. Stupidly, but not knowing it was stupid at that moment, I asked if it was okay if I went in and said hi to them.

Mrs. Gragson said, "Of course."

I did. I spent just three or four minutes in their room—I did know enough to get back out where William was. When I got back to the living room William was sitting on the couch with an empty space for me. I sat down next to him and don't think I said a single word to anyone the hour or so we were there. The adults, especially the women would sneak a look at me every once in a while but all I knew to do was smile at them.

OHHHHHHH it was uncomfortable! For one thing it wasn't really what I thought of as a "party". I mean all they did was sit around and talk—about things and circumstances I knew nothing about.

It occurred to me when I sat down beside William that I probably should not have asked to say hello to Gaylle, especially since she and her sister weren't even allowed out of their rooms during the party—that had probably immediately showed the adults along with William, that I was too young and dumb to be at an adult party. I didn't belong there. I should have been banned to the room with Gaylle and her little sister! I was embarrassed for myself and for William. I was glad when William said we had to leave!

Back with him in his car I felt a little nervous but much more comfortable. He was always the perfect gentleman, fun personality, and, last but not least, a good looking guy. The four blocks back to Mary's flew by more quickly than I would have liked. When we arrived he came around, opened my door and walked me up to their front porch. Of course, the porch light was off which I'm sure was organized by my friend Mary.

William thanked me for going on such short notice and then leaned over and gave me my very first kiss! It wasn't too long, but definitely longer than a quick peck.

Oh my goodness!

My knees were weak and I was afraid I was going to faint! The thought occurred that I never wanted to wash my lips again!

Then he said softly, "Goodnight little cutie. I'll see you later."

And he turned around and left. I fairly floated into the house where Mary grabbed me—Harry Lee was already in bed, but Mary had waited up. She dragged me into the kitchen, sat me down, and grilled me on how it had gone. I was flying high, on top of the world! I can't describe how happy I was! My "prince charming" had actually taken me on a date, my very FIRST DATE, and had KISSED ME ON THE LIPS! My very FIRST KISS! Could life get any better??!! I didn't think so!

I floated on fluffy clouds for two days. On one hand I couldn't wait to see William again. On the other, I was scared because I didn't know how I was going to talk to him or what I'd say! My face would turn blood red just thinking about running in to him. But I did on the third day.

I was walking down Everman Drive with Charlene when William drove up beside us, pulled over and leaned out the window with a big smile on his face looking straight at me not even acknowledging his sister. My heart was pounding. I stood there grinning back not knowing what to say other than "hi".

With a twinkle in his eye he said, "Hey, tight lips, where ya going?"

It took a moment for what he said to sink in. Charlene got it immediately and couldn't suppress a smile. She looked at me and quickly wiped the smile away. I wanted to sink into the ground. Talk about embarrassed and horrified! I couldn't say a word. But my heart felt broken. I knew he liked to tease me but that was absolutely mean! My first kiss and my first date and he was making fun of me in front of another person! I turned around and walked off. Charlene followed. She didn't say a word.

I wondered how long it would be before everyone in the neighborhood heard my new "nickname". I was mortified. But I shouldn't have worried, Charlene never said a word. I should have known she wouldn't. The kids on Everman were good, solid, loyal friends.

But William didn't stop. For the next several days every time he saw me he called me tight lips. It finally stopped hurting and embarrassing me and made me angry! The last time he said it we were in front of several of the neighborhood kids of different ages. He called me tight lips and it got very quiet.

I'd been thinking since the first shock about that insult for several days and had worked hard on what I could say to shut him up!

I looked him straight in the eyes and responded quite loudly so that everyone could hear, "You know William, you knew very well that I'd never been on a date before, which MEANS I'd never been kissed before! If you were ANY KIND OF MAN, you would have TAUGHT ME HOW TO KISS instead of trying to embarrass me in front of everybody!"

He stood there stunned and silent for a couple of minutes and for once his face turned red! Then he turned and walked off. He never called me tight lips again. But we also never dated again. However, I must add that he remained friendly, continued to tease me about other things, and when I went to work a few weeks later he continued to look out for me to make sure no one was bothering or mistreating me. He was a good guy and I'm so glad he was my first date. In that I was blessed.

About the same time of my first and only date with William, Mary started telling me about a family named Springer who had lived in the neighborhood before, moved away—I don't know for how long or why—and were moving back. Apparently, the Springers were related in some way to the Drinnings. The important point that Mary tried to drive home to me was how cute their only boy was.

She kept saying, "Just wait 'til you meet J. W.! All the girls go crazy over him."

But she also talked about two of the daughters, the oldest named Ruth Carol, and the one after J. W., named Jeanie, or "Peanie" as she was called by friends and family. Mary raved about what good people they were and promised me I'd love them.

I admit I was a little curious but didn't get excited about any of it. Mary said they'd lived on Lackey, directly across from Mary and Harry Lee's house, before. She didn't know where they were moving in. It was a month or two before the Springers finally made it back to Everman and I got to meet them.

And yes, Holy Moly! J. W. was a cutie! Every girl on Everman was crazy about him—some silently pining away and some a little more vocal about it.

Mary had been right I did like Ruth Carol and Peanie immediately, and we started hanging out. They had a little sister named Margaret Rose who was about ten and maybe one more even younger that I can't remember.

Ruth Carol was kind of like a "boss" not only of her younger brothers and sisters but of some of the younger girls on Everman, including me. She was probably nineteen or twenty to my thirteen, but just as nice and caring as she could be. Her "bossy-ness" toward us was for our own good. She had a boyfriend named Barry. But she didn't have a job outside her home at that time. It was my understanding she kind of helped take care of the younger Springers and the house. She was good at organizing little fun, social activities for the Everman teenagers. I remember her getting us together at least a couple of times in an empty garage next to their house. She'd plug in a record player and a fan, and some would dance or just listen to the music and laugh and talk. It was a great, innocent time.

I hadn't ever been to dancing parties before so didn't know how to dance and was quite shy about trying. But several people kept encouraging me so I finally got up enough courage one night to get out on the floor with a guy that embarrassed the heck out of me by using mostly his pelvis to "dance" to one of the fast rock and roll favorites. Today, they'd probably call his moves "twerking". Back then it was SCANDALOUS and insulting to me!

I immediately turned and practically ran off the dance floor, hiding behind Ruth Carol. I was so embarrassed and HORRIFIED! Ruth Carol was disgusted and warned all the girls not to EVER dance with that guy again because that's all he could do and it was disgraceful and disrespecting to females. He apparently saw nothing wrong with it. I can't remember who that guy was. I don't know if he was an Everman resident or just a friend of one. I don't think I ever tried to dance at any of the other neighborhood "parties".

And yes, J. W. did ask me out not too long after they moved back into the neighborhood. We went out three or four times but other than being friends we just didn't click. He was a nice, polite, gentleman but a little egotistical—he KNEW he was cute and that girls swooned over him everywhere he went.

Chapter Five

I didn't get to hang out with the Springers, Charlene and Barbara Stockton, or even Mary and Harry Lee much longer. Mama moved us into a cruddy old triplex back up on Everman Drive where Lackey Street dead ended into it. It wasn't even a street, it was an alley! I didn't know until writing this book that those apartments were called "Diaper Alley" by some of the residents. I learned of the nickname from Johnny Ragsdale. He said it was called that because several young girl residents who had gotten married and had babies, moved in there, and every time you drove by you'd see rows and rows of drying diapers hanging on the clothes lines. I don't know if it was called Diaper Alley at the time we lived there but it could have been. My baby sister, Karen was in diapers. We lived in the unit closest to Everman.

That's where we lived when I got serious about going to work. I was sick of the worn, second-hand clothes I'd always had to settle for. I was thirteen and still in the seventh grade. But everybody said I looked much older so I figured I could find a job carhopping which I was eager to do. That looked like a lot more fun than the waitress jobs Mama had toiled at.

Mama advised I'd have to apply for my Social Security card before anyone would consider hiring me. She had to explain what that was. She warned that as soon as I got it I'd have to memorize the number because I'd have it all my life and if I lost it I couldn't work, and I'd have a lot of trouble trying to get a copy. I sent off for it and waited on pins and needles until it arrived. I memorized it immediately.

Two days after I received it I walked several miles up Illinois Avenue to Pete's Drive Inn, a small hamburger joint where I applied for a job as a carhop. I was scared but determined. I was interviewed by Pete, the owner who was probably in his late forties or early fifties. I remember him as being slender, a little taller than my 5' 5", dark curly hair and olive complexion. I told him I was sixteen. He asked me if I'd ever carhopped before and I was honest about that. He hired me for the two weekend days. He told me what to wear: pants, blouse and comfortable shoes, and to be back on Saturday morning.

I was ecstatic. I told all my Everman friends about my new job. When William Stockton heard where I would be working he tried to talk me out of it saying he'd heard some bad things about Pete the owner and didn't trust him. He said the talk was Pete tried to get fresh with the girls that worked for him. I ignored William's warnings.

When I reported for duty, Pete handed me a silver aluminum food tray and told me to go out to the back of the restaurant and practice putting the tray on the window of his car until I was sure I could do it.

When I was confident and reported back inside he put four tall, heavy-duty root beer glasses filled with water, and several plastic burger baskets filled with something on the tray. Then he told me to go back and practice again until I didn't spill even one drop of the water. I did. Then he sent me out to start waiting on cars. The drive inn wasn't that busy, so that day and the ones that followed weren't hard. As long as I was a carhop I never spilled a tray.

The second weekend I worked William came by. I was surprised. He smiled real big when he pulled in and ordered a coca cola. I had no other customers so I stayed to talk to him while he drank his coke. He asked how I liked my job. I told him I loved it.

We did a little more small talk and then he asked, "Is that old man . . ." he nodded toward the soda fountain where Pete sat on a stool at the counter, "leaving you alone?"

I said, "Yes!"

"Well, don't be alone with him," he ordered.

I laughed and told him, "We aren't that busy so I'm inside alone with him a lot. I have no choice!"

"Well, if he tries anything with you, you let me know, okay?"

"Okay." I said, and though I didn't think there was any reason to worry, I did understand that William was trying to look out for me and I appreciated it.

I just wish my mother had been half as concerned as William and my other Everman friends were about my well-being!

I'd only been working at Pete's for a month when a friend of Menard's came by our apartment for a visit. He just happened to be an insurance salesman. Mama, Menard, and he were sitting outside in the front yard of "Diaper Alley" when I came home from work. I had to walk several miles back and forth each day, after walking all day during my shift. I was tired but very happy and feeling pretty grown up and independent, making my own money, saving up to hopefully buy new clothes before school in September.

As I walked toward the front door my mother told me to come over, that I might want to hear what Menard's friend was talking about. I sat down and he started explaining how important it was to have life insurance. I'd never thought about anything like that but he was talking about a policy that was just like a safe savings account. He said after a few years I'd have a bunch of money saved up that I could use for anything I wanted: a car, my own house, a fancy vacation, whatever.

That sounded great but I told him I didn't make enough money to buy insurance. He said it would only be fifty cents a week.

My mother and Menard both rushed to tell me I should do it. "Fifty cents is nothing and just look at all the money you'll have in a few years!

Nobody bothered to mention that I was only making ten to twelve dollars a week, wages and tips combined. Nor why a thirteen year old needed life insurance.

The way the three of them presented it, at that moment, it seemed I'd be stupid not to take the deal. A "pile of money" in a short time? Wow! Besides, it would be a "grown up decision". So I signed up and gave him the first fifty cent payment. Mama and Menard didn't buy a policy—they "didn't have the money". Why they'd talk me into something like that I don't know. Menard was not very bright and completely uneducated but my mother, though not well educated—she quit school in the eighth grade—wasn't stupid. Many years later she obtained her high school diploma, B. A. degree and teaching credential in California with cum laude honors. But even after those admirable accomplishments she continued her entire life to make horrible choices and decisions!

I ended up defaulting on the weekly insurance payments two or three weeks later. I was more interested in clothes and fun at the time, as I should have been.

I only worked at Pete's Drive Inn for two or three more months but William came back several times to check up on me. I was bored stiff at Pete's. We weren't busy enough to earn much in tips, and the days dragged by. My hourly pay rate as a carhop was forty cents. For sixteen hours a week my check before taxes was six dollars and forty cents. Because we had so little business I was lucky to make three or four dollars a day in tips.

I ran into Mrs. Drinning one day on Everman and she told me that she and two of her sisters, Hazel and Frances, who also lived on Everman, were working for a man who owned two drive inns. One was a Dairy Queen on Illinois Avenue just up the street a ways from Pete's, and the other was a Dairy Mart on South Hampton Road in South Oak Cliff which was a long way from where we lived. Mrs. Drinning drove the three of them to work and back every day, dropping Frances off at the Illinois drive inn. She and Hazel went on to work on South Hampton.

Mrs. Drinning said they needed a fulltime day carhop on South Hampton and since she and Hazel cooked and worked the soda fountain, if I was interested I could ride back and forth to work with them. I was interested! School was almost out and I'd have all summer to earn money for new clothes. I rode over with her a few days later and talked to the owner. He hired me, probably because of Mrs. Drinning's recommendation, and because she was going to make sure I got to work every day. I was to start the day after school let out.

That same day Mama moved us to a house on Works Avenue which was on the other side of the Central Expressway.

EVERMAN DRIVE

All my close friends were on Everman but I knew a few kids slightly, who lived on Works because we all rode the same school bus to Wilmer Hutchins. I just wasn't close with any of them.

Many of the teenagers on the Works side of the Central Expressway weren't all that friendly. Some were downright mean! One girl who rode my bus I remember in particular. I know her first name but will not mention it here. She was a Hispanic girl who seemed to take pride in being rough, tough, and mean!

I remember her so well because she decided she didn't like cute, quiet, little Arlene Shepherd that lived over on Everman and worked in her parents' grocery store.

One day this female thug attacked Arlene on the bus with fists and every other trick she had. I doubt very seriously that anything like that had ever happened to Arlene. She was just too nice a girl! But she did try to defend herself. They fought for several minutes. Several of the other students stood up around them and egged it on, or encouraged whomever they wanted to win. The male bus driver pretended he saw and heard nothing which was absolutely impossible. I felt so badly for Arlene. But other than red spots on her face, her pretty, long brown hair a mess, scratches on her face and arms, and her dress all askew, she got up at her bus stop and got off with a lot of dignity.

But the next, day, the day after that, and DAYS after that, the same thing happened! The she-thug jumped Arlene every single day on the bus home for a week at least, maybe more! Arlene knew what was going to happen every day but she hung in there and did her best. The bus driver never made a move or a sound!

I asked Arlene why she didn't tell the school or her parents what was happening but she said she couldn't. If she told the school, people would say she was chicken and she'd never live it down. If she told her parents, she'd get in trouble. So, it continued until the she-thug got bored and trained her sights somewhere else.

One thing I can say, Arlene may not have known how to fight in the beginning, and may not have been the victor in the end, but she DID hold her own, and she never cried. I could tell by her facial expression when the she-thug would finally back off, that Arlene was close to tears, but none ever fell. Nobody who witnessed that atrocity could EVER call Arlene a coward!

Even though I didn't get to hang out with my Everman friends anymore I did meet someone special at The Dairy Mart. Not too long after I started there I met my next boyfriend, Pete Hensley. He was eighteen, worked fulltime at a bakery somewhere in Dallas, and had an old 1950 Ford that was constantly breaking down. With work and seeing Pete when I could, I didn't see much of anyone else—not even my family. I doubt seriously if my mother even knew I'd switched jobs. She was too involved as usual with her own "world".

By that time she'd had Menard's second baby, a little boy she named Terry Lee. She stayed home a couple of weeks after she gave birth and then found a waitress job somewhere. I have no idea who kept the two babies, nor what my two younger brothers did during that time. Menard continued to work for the Sanitation department.

The Dairy Mart was a much better job than Pete's Drive-in. It was a lot busier which meant I didn't get bored and made, even on slower days, at least twice to three times the tips I had made at Pete's. Plus, I liked working with the adult Drinning sisters. But I was by no means rollin' in dough! The hourly rate was still forty cents an hour. After taxes, I got to take home fourteen dollars and fifty cents for forty hours a week, plus whatever tips I could earn. My old boss, Pete, had taught me that the more I smiled, and the better service I gave the customers, the more tips I'd make. I took that to heart and earned the nickname "Smiley". I was pretty popular. My customers, mostly teenagers, liked me and I enjoyed working and kidding around with them.

After the first couple of weeks I was able to start buying new items of clothing. At first it was new Capri's and blouses and a pair of Ked's (washable tennis shoes) because that's what I wore to work. Later on I began to buy dresses and dress shoes for school. I also went as soon as I could to a beauty salon and got my first professional beauty shop haircut and permanent. I had the beautician do my hair in a short "Bubble" which was popular at the time.

The only other time in my life I'd had a haircut outside of home, was in the third grade. I'd finally talked my father into letting me get the new "D. A." haircut that was all the rage. Why I wanted that style I don't know because it really was mostly worn by male celebrities and I always *aspired* to be a "girly girl", except I never had the clothes or accessories.

The D. A. cut was very short, slicked back on both sides, and the back looked like the rear-end feathers of a duck. It was a favorite of movie and rock stars. Its actual name was "Duck's Ass" but people back then didn't say words like "ass" in public, ESPECIALLY in mixed company. Polite people called it the "Duck's Tail", or just used the initials.

Daddy took me to a barbershop because, of course that was cheaper, and maybe because it was actually a man's haircut (although I doubt he knew that. He never went to movies and only listened to country music on the radio). I had gone to the movies every Saturday that we went to town for supplies when Mama and Daddy were together. The cost for kids under twelve was a quarter and there were always two movies and a long section of cartoons. I didn't get money for anything else but I was thrilled with that. So, it was probably in the movies that I discovered the D. A.

After the barber completed my haircut Daddy refused to spend the extra dollar or so for the container of stuff (cream or wax) that you **HAD** to use to get the hair to stay in place ESPECIALLY in the back and on the sides like it was supposed to! Daddy said that was a waste of money! So, I just looked ridiculous for several months—my short hair hanging straight down all the way around looking as if someone at home had taken a deep-bottomed bowl, put it on my head, and cut around it. Daddy ALWAYS ruined everything because he was so CHEAP.

After working a couple of months on South Hampton I was able to buy three or four new dresses for school. I was so proud! My life was going to be a lot different when school started in the fall. I threw the old second-hand-store, plastic melted-jacket in the garbage within a couple of weeks of working. I'd soon be an eighth grader and then I'd be in high school. I wouldn't have to be ashamed of my clothes anymore!

I was able to see Charlene, Ruth Carol, and Peanie on Everman a couple of times that summer. I was so proud of my new clothes I made sure I wore them when I went over. They all complimented me on how I looked. I felt pretty good about my new life even though I had missed them. But they were busy and so was I. So, I and my Everman friends drifted apart. I never saw them again. I saw Linda Drinning a couple of times in the beginning of the eighth grade in the halls of Wilmer Hutchins.

I did get a huge surprise at school though. I'd had no indication all during the seventh grade that any of the teachers knew I was alive except as target practice for Mr. Henderson.

Looking back now I'm sure some of the teachers (and even my classmates) must have wondered what was going on when I normally dressed in my worn second-hand clothes and rundown shoes—then out of the blue I'd show up wearing nice clothes, hair done up in a fancy do, make up on, and sporting a beautiful Mouton coat (which were all Mary's). The inconsistency didn't occur to me then. I just knew I felt like a million bucks when I got to dress up.

But when I returned in the eighth grade I wore nice clothes, not expensive or fancy, but pretty things, every single day. Over the summer I'd been able to buy, in addition to my work clothes, five new dresses for school—one for each day of the week.

I felt great, much more confident and yes, pretty. Within the first week or so I was called into the Principal's office and told I had been chosen to be the office monitor for the last period of the day. That meant I pretty much handled the office alone. I answered the phones, helped or directed students who might come in with problems or questions, and mid period I'd go to each seventh and eighth grade rooms to pick up the class attendance slips that the teachers clipped on the classroom doors.

Years later I'd realize the teachers had probably suggested me for that job because they'd noticed my various attempts in seventh grade (using borrowed clothes and beauty help) and new way of dressing in the eighth grade to better myself. I'd always maintained good grades, even in math. They, more than likely, thought the office monitor position would help to keep me in school. And it would have—if I'd had a choice and any support from home! Boy did I feel special with that seventh period duty! I was on top of the world. I was somewhat popular at school, very popular at work, and now I was looking good and pretty confident.

It was in that atmosphere that I first set my eyes on a cute, new boy in the eighth grade named Johnny. He had short, thick black hair, dark eyes, and was about two inches taller than me. When I'd get to his room for the attendance slip in my capacity as office monitor, I couldn't help it; my eyes went straight to him each time. He'd always be looking straight at me. During our short recesses he'd stand close to where I was but we didn't ever get up enough courage to talk to each other more than to say hi and smile. I was still working. I'd switched to night shift, and as soon as I got off the school bus I'd get on the city bus and head to work. I was also still "going steady" with Pete, and felt like it wasn't right to get too friendly with Johnny.

As it turned out, it wouldn't have made any difference anyway. Mama moved us way out into the country, in the middle of nowhere, about the second month of the eighth grade. I was out of school completely for a couple of weeks. We were so far out in the boonies I was very afraid I wouldn't be able to find a way to work and that would have shattered my world.

Menard came up with a solution. He said he'd drive me to work for five dollars a week for gas, but I'd have to find my own ride home every night because he wasn't willing to get out of bed at midnight to go get me. Keep in mind a gallon of gas at that time was twenty-eight cents! AND, my total weekly paycheck was fourteen dollars and fifty cents! Depending on the night of the week and how busy we were my tips could be three dollars or twelve to fifteen dollars. Menard's "deal" was my only choice. I wasn't willing to give up my "life-line" to a world of normal people who laughed, had fun, and treated me like a human, OR let go of my income!

I gave Menard the five dollars but disliked him even more if that were possible. Again, Mama said nothing and apparently didn't give a thought as to how I'd get home in the middle of the night. Thankfully, Pete drove me home most of the time, but there were times I'd have to ask one of my regular customers if they'd give me a ride home and I'd offer a dollar or two for gas. I shudder now to think how dangerous that could have turned out because I didn't know those guys at all! And that would come home in a horrifying way a few months later.

That move into the country lasted about three weeks. Mama, by that time, was barely civil to Menard which made it much harder for my brothers at home because Menard took out his frustration and anger on the boys. He'd always used the belt on them if he felt like it and Mama never objected.

One night when she was gone, Menard got angry with the boys and started after them with a belt for nothing. I had had enough! I intervened and told him to leave them alone. He turned on me and said he'd whip me just as quick as he would them. I was furious and so sick of him I picked up a tall metal lamp and practically dared him to!

I yelled, "You raise that belt on me and I'll bash your head in, you old S. O. B.!" (Only I didn't use the initials!)

And I meant it. I was scared—he was about six foot one to my five foot five and weighed a lot more than my hundred and twenty pounds, but I was going to give it all I had! My bluff worked. He backed off, threw the belt down and left the house.

I heard him complaining to my mother about it when she returned and he never drove me to work again, but it didn't matter. Mama left him and moved us a day or two later into a tiny, furnished, efficiency apartment off Jefferson Avenue in South Oak Cliff. She didn't do it because Menard had been mean to the boys or threatened me. She was just done with him. She left all of our cheap furniture, dishes, and toys for the kids, etc., and only took a few changes of the kids' ragged clothes.

I made sure I packed and took all my new as well as fairly presentable old clothes! She didn't even tell Menard, or the landlord (this was her usual modus operandi) that we were moving—that had to be a secret. I was glad, but even then I did silently wonder how and why she could just take Menard's two kids away and hide them from him. I didn't care about Menard, but I felt sorry for the babies. I knew how it felt. She'd done the same thing with my father when she married Menard and moved us to Dallas. Granted, Daddy had never been much of a father but he was the only one we had.

But, as evidenced time and time again, just as in this instance, if her ex's could help her with anything (like keeping the boys for a while) she'd get back in touch with them. This wouldn't be the last time she'd run and hide from her kids' fathers. And yet she'd lambast the fathers to everybody who'd listen because she allegedly didn't get any financial assistance from either of them! Poor "innocent victim"!

The good thing about that move to the Jefferson area was that we were much closer to my job on South Hampton. I could ride the bus to work but still had to find rides home every night. I wasn't as thrilled with my job now though. The owner had sold the South Hampton Dairy Mart a couple of months earlier and Mrs. Drinning and her sister had gone back to work for the one on Illinois. I missed Mrs. Drinning very much. I heard my friend Linda Drinning had also gone to work as a carhop on Illinois. And, Pete and I had broken up.

The new owners of the Dairy Mart weren't as friendly or involved as the previous ones had been and they had hired a new carhop for daytime. Her name was Dot and she was the girlfriend of one of the boys who'd lived three houses from me on Works Avenue. Dot was cute and fifteen years old. I didn't know her at all. I hadn't even known her boyfriend or any of his family. The people on Works Avenue weren't friendly, even the ones I knew from the Wilmer Hutchins' bus—they just kept to themselves and so did I.

However, it quickly became apparent that Dot, for unknown reasons, hated my guts! She was rude and mean and no matter how hard I tried to make friends she'd do things to try to get me in trouble or make me look bad.

One weekend the boss was expecting a lot of business so he asked me to come in and work with Dot. No problem for me. But she didn't like it. She started out the day with her haughty, snobbish attitude so I stayed on my side of the carhop lean-to and tried to not pay any attention to it. However, about mid-afternoon we got really busy. The lot was full and both Dot and I were running to deliver the trays of food to the customers. A car that I knew well drove up on my side of the lot. The driver was a fairly regular customer about nineteen years old but he was always sarcastic and smart-alecky. I asked Dot if she'd mind taking that car. She gave me an annoyed look and asked why.

I just said, "He kind of makes me uncomfortable. I don't like to wait on him. I'll catch one of yours if you want me to."

She flounced out to his car and stayed there talking to him a few minutes before bringing his and his girlfriend's orders back and turning them in.

Then she turned to me and said, "He wants to talk to you for a minute."

I said, "Oh no! What about?"

She shrugged and said, "I don't know, he just said to tell you to come out."

So I took out one of my orders and then walked over to his car wondering what in the world he wanted.

As soon as I approached his window he said in a very loud voice, "SO, YOU DON'T LIKE ME HUH?!"

I was shocked and didn't have time to respond. It was obvious Dot had run right out and told him what I'd said, and had probably added a lot to it.

He shouted, "Well I don't like you either, I think you're probably the dumbest cow that's ever worked here!"

Then his girlfriend chimed in. The cars parked around him could hear everything they were saying. I couldn't get a word in edgewise and was embarrassed and humiliated. So I just turned and walked back into the carhop lean-to. Dot was in there cleaning and stacking her trays.

Still in shock, I said quietly, "Why did you do that? I would have NEVER done anything like that to you!"

She threw the tray and the towel down that she had in her hands, turned to face me, with hands on her hips and said in a high, raised voice, "Don't start with me! I won't put up with your sh*t!"

Now I was in double shock!

What was my "sh*t??"

I'd never said a negative, smart, or ugly word to her! I'd tried to make friends but she wouldn't give me a chance. The only thing I could figure out was she had to be jealous because a lot of the customers DID like me. But, they liked her too, so what was the big deal? I didn't get it. But, now I saw she was going to do her best to turn customers against me anyway she could. I turned my back on her and continued my shift. I've wished ever since that I'd gone immediately to the boss and told him what she'd done because she was ruining his business with stunts like that. But at the time it didn't occur to me. I let it go but refused to work the same shift with her again.

Chapter Six

That same week I applied for a carhopping job a few blocks down the street at the Dairy Queen which was three times bigger than the Dairy Mart. It employed two carhops on weeknights and sometimes three on weekends. I was sure I'd make more tips there. I got the job right away. Then I enrolled at Regan Elementary for the rest of that year. Regan was a first through eighth grade school a few blocks away from our rooming house in South Oak cliff.

Mama was working the graveyard shift at Rockyfeller Hamburger Stand on Jefferson a couple of blocks from our apartment. She had sent my two brothers to my father's in Kingston, and baby Terry somewhere twenty-four hours a day. She kept Karen who was crawling but not yet walking, at home on my nights off and made me take care of her. When I worked she was sent to some babysitter. So, one more good reason to work all I could!

During the day, when I was at school Mama would lay the four dining room chairs on their sides and tie them together in a circle. She'd lay a quilt or blanket on the floor inside the circle sort of like a play pen and put Karen inside that while she slept. When Karen cried Mama would wake up and feed her then put her back in the pen and go back to sleep. We lived there for about two months. I'm sure the reason we moved from there was because the other tenants were complaining of Karen's crying.

Then Mama found a woman's name and phone number in the newspaper who was advertising day care. She went and talked to her and came back, packed up Karen and Terry's clothes and took them back to the woman, whose name was Dora. She left the two babies there twenty-four hours a day, seven days a week, for the next year or so. Dora lived on the other side of Dallas, a very long city bus ride from us involving two transfers and waiting times. It took approximately an hour and a half to get there. We couldn't afford a car. The bus was our only option.

Still Mama hid from Menard out of disgust or pure meanness, maybe a little of both. She always made up her own rules. He had no way of finding us. Dallas was a big city even back then. We never had a phone so there was no phone book listing and we moved so often nobody could keep up with us.

The first couple of weeks Mama made the trip to see the babies for an hour or so on Saturdays. But, admittedly, she was working a lot of double shifts at Rockyfellers, the trip over there and back even if she only stayed an hour, took four hours or more. Plus, she was tired most of the time. That's one thing I'll give her—she was a very hard worker and she never had friends—unless she found a boyfriend—so work was about her only option. Very quickly—maybe after the third weekend or so, the trips to see the babies thinned out to more like once a month for an hour, and after that to whenever she felt like it.

Because her visits were so few and far between both babies started calling Dora, Mama. I know that because I went with Mama to visit them a couple of times. My brothers were still at Daddy's in Kingston, so Mama moved the two of us, as soon as the babies left, into a different furnished room with a hot plate in a rooming house a couple of blocks from my school. I rarely saw her but that was nothing new. We lived there for three months until Mama got to know a Rockyfeller coworker named Agnes and learned there was an empty apartment where she lived. It was in a two story rooming house, completely furnished, on Waverly Street just a half block off Jefferson, two blocks from Sunset High School. Again, it was a few blocks closer to the bus stop I used to get to work.

By that time both Agnes and Mama was working relief at several of the different Rockyfeller stands that were situated all over Dallas. The Waverly apartment was very convenient to various bus lines going all over. Agnes lived on the second floor that had hers and the empty apartment, and two separate bedrooms.

We moved into the apartment across from Agnes and her baby son, Andy. Ours and Aggie's apartment were just alike, situated on opposite sides of the second floor. The apartments were three, small "shotgun" rooms; a living room, a bedroom, and a kitchen. The bathroom, shared by the entire second floor, had a large tub, commode, and small sink. It was positioned out in the hall between ours and Aggie's apartment.

She introduced us to the woman and the man who were renting the two separate bedrooms which were positioned to the right of the stair landing with the doors facing each other. The woman's name was Marty. She was in her early thirties and was also working part time at Rockyfellers. She had a funny, different accent and I learned she'd recently moved to Dallas from South Carolina. She seemed strange because when not working and wearing the standard Rockyfeller uniform: a black A-line skirt, white blouse with black string "tie" at the collar and black shoes with white socks, she wore men's clothes.

Because of my love of pretty clothes and makeup I couldn't understand why any female would choose to dress and look like that. Mama said Marty was a lesbian but didn't explain what that was except that she didn't like men. I'd never heard of anybody like that before. I was still perplexed. If she didn't like men, why did she dress like one?!

The man in the second bedroom was someone Marty had met and was trying to help. His name was Dan. He was very thin, in his early forties, and suffered from epilepsy so he couldn't work. He had seizures often. I witnessed several just in the first few weeks of moving there. They were so violent a person could get hurt just being too close to him. Marty would ram a spoon into his mouth to keep him from swallowing or biting off his tongue. Those seizures were scary. Although both he and Marty were nice I stayed away from them as much as I could.

From the point that we moved in on Waverly EVERYTHING in our lives got much worse!

It wasn't the house, I liked it there okay. And I liked Aggie. She was a natural pale blonde with short, thick hair and blonde eyebrows, about twenty-eight years old. Andy was eighteen months old. She'd never been married and the baby's father had deserted her when he found out she was pregnant. She was on her own struggling to survive. But she loved that little boy! However, she had to work almost as much as Mama did just to make ends meet.

When she and I were home at the same time we spent a lot of time together. I saw her as a friend, and spent more time in her apartment than ours. I wasn't home much either. I volunteered to work double shifts at the Dairy Queen on weekends. I'd work inside in the soda fountain during the day and outside carhopping at night. When I graduated from the eighth grade I worked doubles almost all summer. I wanted to be near my friends. I couldn't stand being home.

Thank God I'd made friends fairly close to my age at the Dairy Queen! My two best friends there were Billie and Zana. They were normal teenagers. But even so they still were NOTHING like my Everman Drive friends. These were much more "sophisticated" and world knowledgeable. Yes, I worked a lot, worked hard and got tired but I had fun with my friends and mostly teenage customers. We laughed, and talked about our hopes and dreams and flirted with the opposite sex. Completely opposite from home! I think the comradery at the Dairy Queen was the only thing that kept me going.

But some of my D.Q. friends taught me things I shouldn't have known!

Case in point was Raina, age twenty, and Junie age eighteen, two sisters who worked with me. I still had to find my own rides home at night because the busses stopped about nine or ten. I didn't get off until midnight on weeknights and one o'clock on weekends. It could be two in the morning before we got all the cleaning and prep work for the following morning completed. Pete had often taken me home when I'd worked at the Dairy Mart but he was no longer around.

There were a few guys that were always asking to take me home but not necessarily ones I wanted to ride with. A lot of the time I'd give Raina a dollar or two for gas—which she used to buy Redtop beer, an extremely inexpensive beer that came in a very large bottle. Those sisters loved their Redtop and it wasn't long before I decided to try it with them. Soon I was drinking with them once or twice a week and liking it. Some nights I could barely make it up the stairs to our apartment. They liked to tease me about how much I could drink and I, ignorantly, took that as a compliment!

Many times my boss, Junior, who was in his late twenties would drive me home after work. He was a great guy. He was a good looking man, divorced, and had a beautiful red convertible. During the summer he always put the top down and I loved that. He was always the perfect gentleman boss—probably one of the few bosses in my entire working life that I actually liked and respected as a person. When I was forced by circumstances beyond my control to quit the Dairy Queen without notice I felt terrible—still do when that memory comes back—because he was so nice to me.

But one night close to the end of the summer a good looking guy named Tommy who was a regular customer asked to take me home. I was excited. Tommy had been coming in to the Dairy Queen long before I went to work there and he knew most of the employees. I'd noticed him right off and he'd talked and flirted with me a few times. I had stars in my eyes! Tommy was about five foot ten, built kind of stocky and sported a blonde crew cut. He dressed very well, drove a brand-new silver Chevy Impala and conducted himself in a manner that let everyone know he came from a well-off family. He was also a "college man", meaning he was on his way to a big college somewhere at the end of that summer. Not a lot of the teenagers I knew had the opportunity to go to college—heck, most of them had quit high school for one reason or another. So I was super impressed and flattered that he paid attention to me.

Naturally, I said yes. He left and returned when we closed and then waited patiently until I finished cleaning the lot, turned in my tickets and money, and cleaned my trays for the morning shift. When I approached his car he got out, walked around and opened the passenger door for me. He got back underneath the steering wheel and I gave him directions to my apartment. He nodded and pulled out onto South Hampton.

Within just a few minutes I realized we weren't heading in the direction of my home.

"Where're we going?" I asked. I thought maybe we were going somewhere to get a coca cola and talk a few minutes. I wasn't alarmed. Just curious.

"Oh, just taking a ride," he said, smiling and giving my knee a little pat. I thought nothing of it and relaxed into the seat, gazing out the passenger window enjoying the city lights against the dark sky. A few minutes later we were in a deserted area I'd never been before. He pulled off on a dirt road and parked.

"What are we doing?" I asked.

He switched off the engine, turned toward me jerking me into his arms and planted a long, wet kiss on my lips. I was shocked but still not scared. I'd had a lot of guys try to do some parking but they'd usually start off slow and try to work up to it. I'd never had a problem getting them to understand I wasn't "that kind of girl". Normally, all I had to do was say I didn't want to do this and they'd start the car, apologize, and take me home.

"Tommy, I have to get up early in the morning and be back at work," I said. "I need to get home."

He moved closer and jerked me tighter against him.

"How 'bout a little lovin' first. It won't take long," he said.

Now, I was scared!

"I'm sorry, I don't do that!"

I was insulted he would even think that of me. And I'd thought he was such a nice, special guy!

He grabbed my purse from beside me and threw it into the back seat. He still had hold of the back of my neck. I looked around. It was jet-black outside, not a soul within miles. I had no idea which direction civilization was, much less where I lived from here.

"Either put out or get out!" he growled between clinched teeth. He was squeezing my neck so hard my head ached.

I looked at him a moment, refusing to believe he could mean what he was saying. He had an angry look on his face. I looked around again. How was I going to find my way out of there and get home? I burst into tears and turned toward the back seat to reclaim my purse.

He grabbed my wrist and yelled, "Leave it there!"

I was stunned!

He was going to kick me out in the middle of nowhere and rob me too!

"But how am I gonna get home?" I cried.

He didn't answer but continued to squeeze my wrist. I turned to my door and pulled the handle. It opened and the interior light came on.

By that time I was hysterical. I was being given the choice of getting raped or kicked out in the middle of what looked like a bunch of gravel pits, and having my tips from the night stolen! I had no idea where I was or how to find a phone or even a person to ask for help. Of course my choice was to get out but I was scared out of my mind!

Finally he released my wrist and sat back. I put my right foot on the ground to get out but he grabbed my arm again and said gruffly, "Get back in here!"

My heart almost stopped. He wasn't going to let me go!

"Why?" I cried.

"Just get in. I'll take you home."

I kept my foot on the ground not knowing whether to believe him or not.

"Get in! Let's go!" he yelled and reached across me to shut my door.

He turned on the ignition and stomped on the accelerator fishtailing out onto the street.

"What are you?" he sneered. "A virgin?"

"Yes." I answered truthfully. It took me years to learn some questions don't deserve an answer and some information just isn't anybody else's business!

"Then what in the world are you doing carhopping?" he demanded, as if carhopping was the equal to walking the streets for money.

"What else am I supposed to do? I have to work!"

"Forget it!" He sounded disgusted.

He reached around behind him, grabbed my purse from the back seat and threw it into my lap.

I continued to cry silently, out of shock, fear, disappointment, and embarrassment because he'd apparently thought because of my work I was a cheap slut.

Do other people think that? I wondered.

When we pulled up in front of my house he said, "You'd better be careful who you ride home with. The next guy may not be willing to take no for an answer!"

With that he reached across, opened my door and motioned for me to get out. I refused to look at him but managed to croak, "Thank you for bringing me home . . ."

"Yeah, yeah," he growled and burned rubber out on to the main street.

I ran upstairs and cried myself to sleep. I never told anyone about that incident. I was too humiliated. I worried for days that there was something about me that had caused Tommy to think I was easy.

I even asked my two closest friends at work, Billie and Zana, if they thought I looked or acted cheap. They said I just looked young. Of course, they were both eighteen and lorded it over me about being seventeen. But I was really only FOURTEEN!

I did see Tommy again at the Dairy Queen a week later. He barely glanced at me as he drove through. That was the last time he came in on my shift. I did become more careful about who I accepted rides from. Most of the time after that it was Raina and Junie.

At about that same time my two brothers came home. My father had gotten tired of being responsible for them and was afraid he was assisting my mother in going out and having the time of her life while he was straddled with two kids. So he brought them back un- announced and dumped them off.

Mama had worked two shifts in a row and was sound asleep when they arrived. Of course Daddy took her being asleep in the middle of the day as proof that she'd been living the life of luxury while he had been "played a fool". The boys were just caught in the middle. They were ragged, dirty, and hadn't had a hair cut in quite a while even though Daddy had clippers and when he felt like it would cut his father and other relatives' hair for nothing.

It was apparent he hadn't really paid much attention to the boys but then Mama didn't either and probably didn't even pay any attention to how they looked. Daddy hadn't had much to do with the boys their entire lives. He'd sworn every time he got angry at Mama that both boys had different fathers. He was sure Mama had stepped out on him with both of them.

That day Daddy acted like a jackass and stomped out to go back home to Kingston. Nobody said a word to the boys. But then that was the norm their entire lives. They were turned loose in the community again until school resumed. But Frankie, the oldest, only went to school when he felt like it.

I started ninth grade at Adamson High. I only lived two blocks from Sunset High but I was in the Adamson district, which was a good thing because I'd heard that Sunset had even more wealthy students than Adamson. People with money made me feel even more inferior.

Adamson was so large and different from any school I'd ever been to that I was highly intimidated. There were lots of fancy girls with fancy clothes, lots of pretty cars, and snazzy-dressed, superior- acting boys as well. I remember one girl in particular in a couple of my classes that I couldn't stand. Her name was Shannon. She had long golden hair that looked like she had a beautician do it up every morning. She was tall; probably five foot eight, and had the most striking clothes and shoes. It's probably true I couldn't stand her because I was jealous but she also acted like she was Queen of the day and never stooped to even glance at someone like me. That was okay with me because I wouldn't have had anything in common with her anyway.

About the second week I was rounding a corner at Adamson on my way to a class and got a great shock. Across the hall I saw Johnny, the cute eighth grade boy that had moved to Wilmer Hutchins district who I had stared at when I picked up attendance slips the year before.

But he wasn't all that cute anymore! He'd let his hair grow down to his shoulders, it was stringy and greasy looking and he just looked unkempt. I had never seen a boy with long hair at that point. I was horrified. He saw me too and we both just stood there a minute. I didn't say anything. I continued down the hall and wondered what in the world had happened to him? He had been such a dreamboat last year. Now, I wouldn't want to be seen with him. I saw him briefly a couple more times but we never stopped to talk. Off and on over the years I've regretted not saying something. He may have had a family like mine and just needed a kind word.

It wasn't long until cold weather started blowing in—I don't think I'd even had time to receive a report card. I was extremely unhappy and definitely out of my element at Adamson. But the capper was I'd thrown away, months before, my only jacket; the old melted plastic one and hadn't bought another, so the walk, or bus ride—if and when I could afford it—was very cold. I was okay at work. Junior had purchased several different sizes of heavy duty jackets with the D Q logo on the back and left front pocket and we changed into one of those for our shifts. However, we weren't allowed to take them home. All I had to keep me warm when off duty was a medium-heavy sweater. Good new coats were thirty dollars and more. On my income that was a lot of money. I refused to even think about going into a second hand store! So, I decided to quit school. I told Mama and Aggie.

Mama didn't say much except to blame all our problems on Daddy.

"You could have been something if he'd acted like a father should've," she declared.

I'd hear that a lot over the next several years and each time I'd think, *well does that mean I'm nothing now?*

It always hurt to hear her say that. She might have meant I was smart enough to have been able to make something of my life if I'd had any support—and that was true. I was always an A student. I wondered why she couldn't see that she contributed just as much, and later even more, to the dysfunction and sickness of our family. But she never took on any of the blame and just kept getting worse and worse.

Aggie begged me not to quit. She warned me I'd have to live like she and my mother were; working themselves to death doing double shifts, doing without, watching their kids do without. I didn't listen. I just wanted OUT of Adamson High School and away from the snobs. I did think about what quitting school would mean for my future—I'd never become the writer I'd wanted to be since fifth grade and that depressed the heck out of me for a long time. But then I convinced myself that that dream, coming from a family and station in life like I did, could never have happened anyway. My hatred of the way I felt every day at Adamson, along with my desire to hang out with my friends, won out over everything else.

So, I volunteered to work double shifts as often as possible. Another positive about working doubles was that back then when you worked in restaurants you got at least one meal free each shift, but you couldn't take left overs home. My brothers were at home eating dry bologna sandwiches and cold cereal WHEN they had milk. We even had bologna sandwiches for Thanksgiving that year. Mama would take home hamburgers once in a while. The boys were completely on their own.

It was weird but not long after my brothers came back both Marty and Dan, the two people that rented the two single bedrooms, put padlocks on the outsides of their doors. They didn't say anything to anybody but I wondered why. None of us had EVER locked our doors. I don't know if Mama even noticed. A couple of weeks later Marty and Dan were gone without a word to any of us. Marty had even quit Rockyfellers.

Since nobody ever came to check on the rentals there (I never knew where the adults paid the rent), and since the two boys were sleeping on the fold out couch, and Mama slept in the only bed in the one bedroom where she was sometimes joined by her brand new boyfriend, Gene. I took my few things and put them in the room that had been Marty's.

There was an old double bed, a chest of drawers and a small closet in there. I figured if anyone came and said anything I could always pay a month's rent—I might have to do it in payments—and then promptly move back into our apartment.

No one ever came. And it was SO MUCH more peaceful! I could actually sleep without being disturbed or asked to move. I could listen to my music and dream my dreams. I loved my room. I had put a clock radio on layaway at the Jefferson Street Western Auto store so I could have some music. It took me about six weeks at two or three dollars a week to pay it out. The day I picked it up I put a Hi Fi stereo on layaway. The stereo was a lot more expensive and it would take longer to pay it out but I loved music! I was so proud of my radio and couldn't wait to get my Hi Fi paid off and at home. I was making a list of the records that I loved listening to on the jukebox at work. I was planning on buying a couple of 45's at a time. But first things first!

I didn't even think about a lock for my room. Marty and Dan had taken theirs with them. We'd never locked any house or apartment we'd lived in. And we'd never had a problem. In those years it was strange that anyone would even think about locking doors.

House on East O'Neil Street
Greenville, Texas
Where we lived when
mama met Menard.

Front left Linda Horton age 11, front right Frankie age 7, Back Gary Horton age 5. Weekend at Dad's.

Arlene Shepherd, Gaylle Gragson, Linda Drinning

Photo courtesy of Gaylle Gragson Gregory

Gaylle Gragson, Mr. Murray (Linfield Crossing Guard), Linda Drinning.

Photo courtesy Gaylle Gragson Gregory

Top Left Linda Drinning, Linda Horton, Edgar Horton
Bottom Left Gary Horton, Frankie Horton.
Weekend at my dad's.

Nelda Drinning took the picture.

Betty ?, Linda Horton, and Linda Drinning

Photo courtesy of Gaylle Gragson Gregory

Linda Horton's 13th birthday party in Kingston, TX

DAIRY MART

2739 S. Hampton   Fe-7-9191

Oak Cliff: Dairy Mart
2739 S. Hampton, Dallas, TX.
This was my 2nd car hopping job at age 14.
The carhop workroom is located to the right of photo.

This is a public photo found on Flickr.com by "Coltera"
Licensing is found at creativecommons.com

Harry Lee Drinning, Jr
Photo courtesy of Linda Drinning Van Briggle

LINDA HORTON

Dallas Girl Dies, Three Injured as Car Rams Trees

A 16-year-old Dallas girl was killed and three persons were injured Tuesday afternoon when a new sports car rammed two trees near Cedar Hill.

Killed was Margaret Rose Springer, 16, of 4152 Everman.

Brenda Kay Burkett, 16, of 4218 Everman, was injured and listed in critical condition late Tuesday night at Methodist Hospital.

The driver, Lawrence Austin Jr., 20, of Attalla, Ala., was listed as fair. Homer Henry Neven, 18, of Harding, Mont. was in good condition. Both were transferred to the hospital at Carswell Air Force Base.

Dallas County deputy sheriffs said both young men were stationed with the Air Force at Duncanville.

Capt. Pat McEntee said Austin apparently lost control of the high-powered car headed southeast on Straus Road near State Highway 1382. The car skidded into an embankment, knocked down a tree 16 inches in diameter and smashed into a cedar tree some 40 yards away.

All occupants were thrown out.

McEntee said Austin walked to a nearby house for aid.

The 1966 model car had been driven only 900 miles.

Linda Horton age 16 in California. Wanted to try dark hair.

Chapter Seven

And then I met John at work. He sported a short brown flat-top, had dreamy blue eyes and was just the slightest bit shy. It was well known around the D. Q. that his parents were quite well off and gave him a generous allowance to do as he pleased. His pride and joy was a beautiful, two-tone '57 Chevy. He was a clean-cut college boy who had just broken up with his girlfriend and guess who she was?! The snobby, golden-haired girl named Shannon at Adamson that I couldn't stand!

It was hard to believe that John would ask me out but he did and I was on cloud nine! The first few times, he just took me home from work but one night he took me to a drive-in movie. He was a gentleman, opening doors and making sure when we walked that I was on the inside of the sidewalk—which was proper "etiquette" back then. I was hooked.

About a month after we started dating he took me to his house on Sunday afternoon to meet his parents. They were nice enough and his house was something out of one of those fancy house and garden magazines. I'd never been inside a house like that. They left me alone in the living room for a few minutes. I didn't move from the couch but I tried to memorize every detail to describe it to my friends.

When John and his parents returned we didn't stay long. He took me straight home. I could tell he was upset but he wouldn't say what was bothering him. He barely pecked me on the cheek and drove away.

We were supposed to go out again my next night off but the night before he picked me up at work and when we got to my house he turned off the engine. He said he had something to tell me.

"Okay, shoot," I said.

His face was silhouetted by the street lamp across from my house. He was such a dreamboat. I was so lucky.

It took him a few minutes to respond and when he did, he wouldn't look at me.

"I can't see you anymore," he said.

He had both hands on the steering wheel. I could see his eyebrows were knitted together in a frown.

I didn't think I'd heard him right. We'd had such fun the past few weeks. I swallowed hard.

"Why?" I asked.

Maybe he meant he couldn't see me because he was going somewhere for a vacation or something? When I was going steady with Pete he had gone to Tennessee with his parents to visit relatives for a couple of weeks which had seemed like forever.

"My parents think we're too different," he said.

I waited a moment trying to think what that meant. I blurted out the only thing I could think of right away.

"Because you have money and I don't?"

"It's everything," he said in a rush. "You aren't in school, I'm Catholic and you're not, and yeah, I guess the money thing is in there somewhere too. They don't like it that you're a carhop."

He shrugged and continued to look straight ahead, his hands clenched on the wheel.

I felt dirty but through no fault of my own. Tears started coursing down my cheeks.

"Do those things mean to you and your parents that I'm not a good person?" I asked.

"Of course not. It's just that my parents say it won't work out between us because we're too different. But don't feel bad. I think it's mainly because of Shannon, my ex-girlfriend. She and I dated a couple of years and they got kind of attached to her."

OOOOH! Now I REALLY hated that witchy snob! I straightened my shoulders and raised my head.

"Well, pardon me! I don't want to contaminate you any more than I already have! You go right back to fancy-pants Shannon and have a great life, okay!"

I stepped out onto the sidewalk and started to our porch.

He leaned over to the passenger window and called after me in a pleading voice, "Linda don't be like that! I have to listen to my parents."

I kept walking, tears streaming down my face. When I reached the stairs he burned rubber and was gone.

The following weekend he drove through the Dairy Queen parking lot with Shannon sitting so close you couldn't have put a straw between them. I made sure I smiled real big and waved like I didn't have a care in the world. He pulled up beside a couple of other cars and they talked a few minutes before he drove out onto South Hampton. He looked my way only once.

It's just as well, I thought. I didn't want him to see me cry. As a matter of fact I wasn't going to give anyone the satisfaction of seeing me cry again!

That resolution didn't last long.

Mama and Gene had been seeing each other for a few weeks. I didn't see her or him often, but he had spent the night with her a few times when she had the night off. He seemed to be a nice guy; clean, well dressed but not fancy, always smiling and polite. He treated me and my brothers like human beings. I don't know if he had any idea Mama had two babies farmed out and I sure wasn't going to mention them. I didn't want to chance her anger. I knew nothing about Gene. But I was glad that he seemed several steps above Menard.

He had been there one day the last week when I'd been leaving for work wearing my old sweater. He walked down the stairs behind me and said that I should go back and get my coat that it was very chilly outside.

I didn't go into detail but did say something like, "Oh, I've got to get a new coat; I just haven't had a chance. But I'll be okay when I get to work. They provide Dairy Queen Jackets for us."

"You're gonna freeze before you get to work, Kiddo!" he argued.

"Nah, I'll be okay," I said, knowing exactly how I'd feel out there! I'd been wearing that sweater ever since fall.

When we got outside he headed to his car. I started down the street toward my bus stop.

"You need a ride?" he asked.

"Naw, I catch the bus at the corner. I'm fine," I said, and kept walking.

He made a U turn and headed out to Jefferson Avenue. When he passed me he threw up his hand in a wave and I did the same.

I forgot all about it!

I got home that night at two a.m. and went to bed in my bedroom. When I got up about noon the next day Mama and the boys were gone. I went over to see if Aggie was home but she was gone as well.

I lazed around a little while and then took a leisurely bath before getting ready for work. It wasn't often that any of us got to take our time in the bathroom.

After getting dressed I went in to our apartment see if there was anything in the refrigerator; but nope, not a thing. As I closed the fridge I heard a knock on one of our doors—we always had to look because it always sounded like our door whether it was or not. Truthfully, the only person who visited was the Rockyfeller boss to pick up Mama or Aggie for an emergency shift. It couldn't be a resident because we didn't knock, we just called out whoever's name we were looking for. I made my way to the front door which was open and there was Gene.

"Hey Kiddo! Is your mama home?" he asked with a big smile.

"No. She must have had to work today," I said. "She was gone when I got up."

"Oh," he said. "I thought she was off today."

"I think she was supposed to be but anytime somebody calls in sick, the boss comes to get either her or Aggie to fill in. Aggie's gone too. They might have gone together," I answered.

"Oh well, I was in the neighborhood," he said. "I thought I might take her out for a hamburger."

I shrugged. He turned to go but then stopped and turned back.

"Hey, why don't we go real quick and get you a coat?" he asked.

I was a little embarrassed but said in a cheerful voice, "No, that's okay. I'm gonna get one. But I don't quite have enough money yet. I will soon though."

"Well, let's go right now! I can't get too fancy but I can't stop thinking about you being out there in nothing but a flimsy sweater. It's on me."

"Oh no!" I said.

Now I was really embarrassed. I didn't like for people to know my personal problems and didn't like to accept charity—especially from strangers. I liked being independent and wanted to be able, although I wasn't at that point yet, to take care of myself.

"Oh come on! There's no strings attached. I don't feel right knowing you're out on these streets without a coat. I was gonna tell your mama that today, but since she's not here, I'll just take you and we'll get it. Consider it an early Christmas present... or birthday, Fourth of July, whatever!"

His grin was from ear to ear and his eyes twinkled. He seemed a little embarrassed. I don't think he was used to being something of a "Santa Claus" to someone he didn't know very well. But then I wasn't used to it either.

I'd never had anyone offer something like that. Especially something brand-spanking new! I stood there considering the offer for a moment but it didn't take long to remember how cold it was outside.

I smiled at him and asked, "Are you sure . . . ?"

"Heck yeah! Let's go. You've got a little time before work, right? I'll wait for you in the car."

He started down the stairs with a big grin and his shoulders back. I ran into the apartment, smoothed my hair, put on the old sweater and then ran down the stairs after him. I couldn't believe how nice he was. My own daddy wouldn't even think about taking me to get a new coat, or anything else for that matter. *Wow!* I was excited.

He took me down on Jefferson. Neither of us knew where to go so he parked and we walked until we found a department store that had coats and jackets in a reasonable price range.

He told me to pick out what I wanted and he'd wait for me up front. I was in awe. Nothing like this had ever happened to me. I looked and touched everything in my size in the coat department. I tried on several fake furs reminiscing about Mary and her pretty Mouton. I loved those but decided it wouldn't do since I had to stand and wait at bus stops every day—rain would wreck it. Also, those were a little more expensive. Since I wasn't paying for it I knew I should be cost conscious.

I picked out a blue quilted car coat with a hood for $39.99. It wasn't my favorite but it would do just fine. Warmth was what I was looking for. The saleslady said the color did wonders for my eyes. I mostly cared that it was washable. I could take care of it at the Washateria which was a heck of a lot cheaper than a dry cleaner.

I took the coat to Gene.

"You did good, Kiddo!" he crowed.

He took it over to the cash register, paid for it, handed it to me to put on and then drove back home and dropped me off. I thanked him profusely and promised I'd pay him back for it as soon as I got a little more money ahead.

He reached over, tousled my hair and grinned.

"It's a gift, Kid! No pay-back expected or wanted! Ain't anyone ever given you a gift?"

"No," I said softly but didn't really mean for him to hear that. If he did, he didn't respond. He changed the subject and said something about having to find Mama and maybe take her for lunch her next day off.

I thanked him again and got out.

"Just stay warm okay? And don't work too hard."

With that he drove away and I ran into the upstairs bathroom to admire my new coat in the mirror.

Because of our work schedules I didn't see Mama until about a week later. Gene brought her home from work and they were fighting. I made myself scarce closing the door to my bedroom and listening to my new radio.

After a while I decided to take a bath and then I was going to go to bed. I opened my door with my night clothes in my hands and started across the hall landing trying to be quiet. Our apartment door was open. Mama and Gene were sitting on the sofa talking, still not acting very friendly to each other. They were sitting apart and both their faces were solemn.

I'd hoped to sneak by without being noticed but Gene looked up and said, "Hi Kid, how ya doin'?"

Mama didn't look up.

"Fine," I whispered. I headed on into the bathroom. As I ran the water and bathed I could hear the argument escalating. I wondered what the problem was.

As I started back to my room dressed in my night clothes, dirty clothes in a ball under one arm, I saw Mama and Gene standing near the door, Gene looking as if he was leaving.

He looked at me.

"How's that coat working out?" he asked.

"Great! Thank you," I answered enthusiastically. "I'm not freezing anymore!"

I smiled at him. I still couldn't believe he'd done that for me.

Then I caught sight of Mama's face, hell's fury written all over it. I ducked my head and started for my room again.

"Are you trying to sleep with him?" she screamed.

Who is she talking to?

I whipped around to look and see if there was someone behind me. But she was staring at me, livid with anger!

I looked at Gene, not believing she really meant me! He was looking down at his shoes. What little I could see of his face was blood-red.

I looked back at Mama. Her eyes were like ice, boring into me.

"What?" I stammered.

What is wrong with her?

But she screamed it again, adding, "Because if you are, just tell me and I'll butt out!"

I couldn't speak and began to cry.

She thinks I want her boyfriend . . . over a piece of clothing?! My own mother thinks that I want to "sleep" with her boyfriend . . . a man old enough to be my father?! How can she think that? What have I done?

Gene doubled his fist and looked like he wanted to hit her, but he didn't make a move. In a low voice filled with anger he said, "How dare you say something like that!"

He turned to be sure he was facing her spot on and that she had to focus on him.

I couldn't say anything. I was paralyzed in that spot.

"The kid was cold. You didn't do anything about it! I was just trying to help out. Neither one of us has done anything wrong, but YOU . . . you're about as wrong as a person can get!"

He forced his hand down by his side and flexed it open and closed, open and closed.

I felt sick. In my stomach and my heart. I turned and ran to my room, locking the door from the inside. I heard more shouting, Gene's footsteps running down the stairs and then the lower level front door slammed shut. I cried myself to sleep.

When I awoke the next morning, I knew my life would never be the same. Mama had done and said a lot of rotten things in my life but she wouldn't be able to even try and take this one back. AND SHE DIDN'T. In the years to come she'd even deny it ever happened. But it affects me from time to time, even to this day, many, many years later.

From that day on I stayed away from home even more. I was hanging out with my friends and started staying overnight at their houses. Sometimes I'd be away three or four days in a row and Mama didn't seem to notice or ever ask where I'd been.

Gene never came back after that night. Mama was back to working and sleeping. Frankie and Gary were still on their own.

One day when I was at home I overheard Mama talking to Aggie. She said she'd called my father and asked him to take the boys again but he'd refused. Then she went on to say that the woman who had the two babies wanted to adopt Terry Lee.

"What about your little girl?" Aggie asked. She had never seen either baby so she didn't know their names.

"No, they had two girls who are now grown. They want Terry because they want a son."

"What are you going to do?" Aggie asked.

"I don't know," she said.

"Are you thinking about it?" Aggie asked with a hint of incredulity in her voice?

"Well, if they wanted both of them it might be a little easier to make a decision," Mama said. "I hate to think about splitting them up."

I didn't want to hear anymore. She was still keeping where we were and how his babies were doing a secret from Menard. She apparently wasn't even going to give him a chance to know what was going on. Did he care? I didn't know that. I felt sick at my stomach. She was trying to get rid of Frankie and Gary again. She'd tried a couple times earlier just before I got the job at the Dairy Mart to get her mother's sister in Sulphur Springs—the one we used to barge in on for Thanksgiving or Christmas dinners—to take me! When Aunt Vera said she just couldn't be responsible for a teenage girl, (Her kids were all grown and she was old—just a few years younger than Mama's mother) Mama did her best to make it seem like Aunt Vera was just being selfish and didn't care what happened to any of us.

Mama seemed to look at us kids like we were a litter of unwanted kittens.

How could she even think about giving up her babies?

I didn't hear my name that day but if she could so easily discuss getting rid of the other four, I wouldn't be far behind especially because now she was afraid I'd go after her boyfriends! I was nervous, but on the other hand I could take care of myself. I'd already proven that, hadn't I? She wasn't going to send me anyplace I didn't want to go! But I didn't make enough to pay rent anyplace on my own so what could I do?

What I thought *MIGHT* be the answer came not too long after that. I hated to leave my Dairy Queen friends but I wanted to make more money. That opportunity came very quick. Mama's Rockyfeller boss, Mr. Glasscock, came by to pick her up for an extra shift and said that he had an opening for another relief waitress if I was interested. He explained it paid eighty cents an hour—double what I made as a carhop—plus tips. And all the stands were pretty busy so I could probably pull in some good tips.

He added, "However, I wouldn't put you on the same shift with your mother or Aggie because I don't think that would be a good idea. But we have locations all over town so you'd be working full time, especially if you were willing to take on a grave yard shift now and then."

Making more money was what I was looking for. I told him I'd think it over and get back to him. I talked it over with my D. Q. friends, Billie and Zana. Neither of them had ever been inside a Rockyfellers but Zana said right off, "Oooooh, that doesn't sound like a place I'd want to work. It sounds boring."

Billie was a little interested. She was gearing up to start Beauty School in a couple of months. She wanted more money too but she only had certain hours she could work.

I mulled it over a couple of days and made the decision. I called the Rockyfeller boss and told him I'd take it. He said he'd put me on the schedule to start in ten days—which is the length of time I gave Junior for my notice.

I donned the black skirt, white blouse and white socks with tennis shoes and went to work at Rockyfellers. Mr. Glasscock sent me all over Dallas to different stands. I had to ride the bus of course and some of the locations took an hour and a half or so to get to. I trained to do everything; wait on the counter, prep the food, make cold sandwiches, wash dishes. I learned to grill the various foods; hamburgers, and breakfast. The three I worked at most often was the one just down the street from our apartment near Sunset High School, the one in Edgefield, and the one located in Walnut Hill which was my longest bus ride, at least an hour and a half one-way.

The one near Sunset required only one employee per shift. Most of the others needed at least two. I liked working alone but I liked Walnut Hill best because it was the newest and nicest, and looked out across a portion of Bachman Lake. I'd sit at the window on my lunch break staring out at the lake, listening to "Stranger on the Shore" by Mr. Acker Bilk, "Please Release Me" by Little Esther Phillips, and "Born to Lose" by Ray Charles. I played those three songs on the jukebox every day I worked there. And although I loved Ray Charles' song I refused to identify with the words, "born to lose". I didn't know how but believed, even though I'd quit school, someday, somehow I was going to make something of myself!

When the newness of my job wore off, which took place almost as soon as training was over, I became bored. Most of the customers were older people and they just weren't as much fun as the teenagers at the Dairy Queen. Plus, the tips were terrible! Yes, I made double my hourly rate but the adults didn't even tip as well as the teenagers.

Chapter Eight

The one bright spot of working at Walnut Hill was I got to meet a cute eighteen year old guy named James who would come in on the graveyard shift and hang out with Aggie. Aggie had introduced him to my mother and they'd talk and joke with him during the slow times while they did their side work. Aggie told him about me and he came in on my shift one day—I guess to "check" me out. I didn't think much of it. Then he came in again and again, but I didn't say much more than hi, and take his order for coffee. I was still pretty shy and would in no way be the one to be assertive; girls just didn't do that back then. If you did, you were accused of "chasing boys". It was the guy who had to initiate the relationship.

Speaking of relationships, one weekend day when I was trying to reconcile myself to missing my D. Q. friends and working in a boring job, I got a huge surprise! Mary, my dearest friend from Everman showed up at my apartment out of the blue! How she found me I don't know but when I saw her I thought it had to be some sort of miracle. I don't know if I even asked her how she found me. We still didn't have a phone so no phone book listing and I hadn't seen or talked to anyone from Everman since I'd last seen Mrs. Drinning at The Dairy Mart. That had been at least a year, maybe longer.

Mary showed up alone. She'd gotten her drivers' license and was in a car I'd never seen. I must have seen her pull up because I remember she didn't come into our apartment. Instead, I got into her car where we sat and talked a little while. I was so excited to see her. But it took only a few minutes to notice she'd undergone a huge change. She wasn't the same Mary I'd known. She'd gotten very religious and that's mostly what she wanted to talk about. For me, it was uncomfortable. She talked about how I needed to be going to church and learning about Jesus, etc. But I had negative memories of church. Mama had dragged me to fundamental church services sporadically when I was little and those meetings had scared me every time! The attendees would run around the building, jump, fall down on the floor, wave their arms in the air, cry, scream, etc. I would be a nervous wreck when we'd finally get to leave.

Later beginning when I was about seven, Mama invited Mormon Missionaries into our home once a week and then dragged us to Mormon Church services for a few months. That church was also very different and a little spooky to me—however they were just the opposite of the fundamentalists. The Mormons were extremely quiet and reverential inside their chapels. But some of the things we were taught in the children's classes were foreign to me. Believe it or not, my mother became a children's Sunday school teacher in that church. I was proud of her for that.

But before long they literally kicked her out for something my father accused her of—I don't know if the "banishment" was temporary or forever. I was too young to know all the details. The church leaders had apparently obtained enough evidence to believe the accusation. I didn't know back then what Mama had done, or even if she had done anything, to get kicked out of the church. For many years she claimed it was all a lie made up by my father and his family. And it did happen at about the same time as their divorce and the court hearing. Daddy, from my earliest memories, was always accusing her of things so

I just accepted that he might have made something up just to get revenge on her—he wasn't above making up lies himself!

However, many decades later when I got involved heavily in genealogy research, trying to determine why my family was so screwed up, I found a hand written letter by my mother that explained everything.

I'm sure Mama had thought that letter would never be read by anyone but her intended addressee. But it turned up several years after my paternal grandmother's death in a box of old photos and twenty or more letters from my father to his parents when he was in the army stationed at Fort Ord, California for basic training, and then from the Philippines.

Grandma had saved that box of stuff for years, including the letter written by my mother. That box had wound up in the possession of Grandma's daughter, Ruby. I doubt if Ruby had ever even read the letter or any of the others. She wasn't interested in family tree stuff. But just before Ruby's death, even though I'd only seen her once in about thirty years, she sent me the box to help with my genealogy search.

It will serve no purpose here to reveal the information in the letter. Plus, there's a huge chance of sullying the reputation of a possible innocent person—but my father was telling the truth! The church had good reason to excommunicate her! I still have that letter in my records.

Church wasn't a positive thing for me so, when Mary started talking about Jesus and sin after not seeing her for so long, I got very nervous. I wanted the "old Mary" to resurface; my friend and confidant. I realize now she cared enough about me to want to share her faith. She probably thought a relationship with Jesus would help me with my terrible home life and horrific role models—and it probably would have. But that day, I just thought she'd gotten weird.

We talked in her car for about thirty minutes and then she had to go. That was the last time I saw her. But definitely NOT the last time I thought about her and Harry Lee!

A couple of nights later I got home from work very tired and looking forward to kicking back and relaxing. When I got upstairs I went to turn on my radio and discovered one corner was broken completely off and the clear plastic cover over the clock face was shattered. Nothing else was out of place in my room.

I stormed into the apartment but the boys were sound asleep. I was furious but couldn't get them awake enough to find out what had happened. I stomped back to my room and turned the radio on. At least it still worked. But once again I cried myself to sleep! It had taken me several weeks to pay for that radio. Now it was broken and ugly. It seemed like everything in the world was against me! And nobody cared.

The next morning I learned Frankie and Gary had been wrestling in my room and had knocked the radio off the nightstand. Mama refused to do anything about it. She just pursed her lips and set her jaw and said nothing. That enraged me even more! She let the boys act like little savages, let Frankie miss school and hang out who knew where, let him bully Gary around constantly, didn't even provide enough food for them! It did no good to try to talk to her. She did only what she wanted to do and ignored everything else.

My radio was the last straw. I went out immediately when the stores opened and bought my own padlock for my room. Anger began to build inside me. And then I'd get depressed. My life was horrible. I had no future. I wasn't good enough for a lot of people. I had nothing and it looked like I'd never get ahead. There certainly wasn't anything to look forward to.

Aggie put a lock on her door right after that.

And like a stupid kid I decided I'd get back at Mama. I knew exactly how. Daddy was a smoker. He'd always rolled his own cigarettes, Prince Albert brand. Mama hated smoking.

I'd heard her say many times, "I'll tell you one thing, Linda better not smoke, but if she does she better do it in front of me. She'd better not sneak around!"

So, I was going to show her! I tried Bel Aires first because they had a pretty package. But they were terrible. Surely, not all cigarettes were like that! Next, I tried Kools because of the name—I wanted to be cool. They were just as bad as the Bel Aires. So I tried Winstons and those were okay. But I had to WORK at liking smoking! However, they did make me feel grown up, and a little bit bad. I'd see grownups look at me with judgmental expressions when I lit up and I'd silently dare them to say anything.

It took a few days but when I finally got the hang of it, I lit up in the apartment one morning right in front of Mama. I had a Mason jar lid on my knee for an ashtray and I lounged back against the sofa cushions and took a deep drag when she walked through on the way to the bathroom. She looked at me long and hard. I waited. I didn't know exactly what I was going to do but I was going to make sure she remembered her words about how I was supposed to smoke in front of her. And, she wasn't going to stop me!

She didn't say a word. She continued into the bathroom, got ready for work and left. And though I kept hoping it would make her feel bad and I'd get a response. I should have known better! Aggie tried to tell me I'd regret it but she smoked so I didn't listen. I smoked from then until 1983, *absolutely* regretting it after a couple of years. Quitting was one of the hardest things I ever did.

One late Saturday night I trudged up the stairs to my room and noticed all the lights were on except my room which was padlocked. That was very unusual. Something had to be going on.

When I got upstairs I saw the door to Aggie's apartment was open. I could hear voices coming from inside. The door to our apartment was closed. I opened it and started inside when Aggie's voice rang out, "Hey, Linda. You got a minute?"

I turned and was not surprised to see her and Andy, her little son balanced on one hip, wide awake and grinning at me, his two new teeth gleaming. Aggie still had on her uniform.

"Yeah, sure," I stopped, turned around and went toward her. I figured she was going to ask me to babysit while she went out for a little while. I was tired and hated babysitting! I'd had too much of that with my siblings already! I wasn't even sure I'd ever want kids of my own! But, little Andy was a cute kid and I liked Aggie so I would do it for a little while.

She motioned for me to follow into her apartment. I obeyed. Andy cooed and wriggled, slapping his hands on her shoulder, trying to get down. Her hours were so irregular, both she and Andy were ready to go at just about any time, day or night. She hugged him and planted a noisy kiss on his nose and said, "Nuh-uh Buster, it's almost your bedtime."

As we entered her doorway I saw a guy sitting on her sofa. He stood and smiled uncertainly. It was the cute guy from Walnut Hill Rockyfellers.

"Linda you've met James, right?" She looked from him to me and back. "He hangs out with us sometimes on the graveyard shift."

"Hi," I managed, looking straight into his eyes as he looked at me. He couldn't decide whether his hands should go in his pockets or rest on his hips. Of course, I remembered him! We hadn't talked but I'd had a few daydreams about him. He had dark brown eyes that reminded me of creamy hot fudge and the rest of him wasn't bad either. He had a neat brown crew cut, full lips, even teeth. He wore sharply creased jeans and a button down, pale blue, short-sleeved shirt. There was a small, faint scar on his chin.

He smiled, reached his hand out to shake and said, "We haven't been formally introduced but we've seen each other before."

Suddenly I remembered I was still in my uniform, complete with a big coffee stain on my white work blouse after a busy Saturday night. I wished a hole would appear in the floor and swallow me up! I must look horrible.

Aggie told us to sit down and we all did. Aggie put Andy down on the floor and gave him a couple of toys to keep him busy. I sneaked a peak at James and got caught. I blushed furiously and tried for the next fifteen minutes to think of something—anything to say—but failed miserably.

All James could think to say was "Well, how was work tonight?"

Aggie tried to make conversation but came across sounding forced so after a few minutes I excused myself telling them I was really tired and needed to go to bed. And I did, but didn't sleep for a long, long time.

At ten thirty the next morning Aggie knocked on my door and invited me to breakfast. "I've got coffee and a good looking guy who rode the bus all the way over here to see you! And, I can scramble some eggs if you're up for that."

"Awwww Aggie, I'm sleepy," I complained. I didn't look my best first thing in the morning.

But she insisted.

"James is a great kid," she said. I've known him for several months. He comes in for coffee and hangs around talking to us during the slow times. He lives with his mom just down the street from Walnut Hill. You'll like him. And I know he likes you!"

She grabbed my hand and tugged. I pulled it back to stretch.

"Come on! He's a sweet guy. He's been trying to get us to introduce him to you for a couple of weeks now."

"I don't know what to talk to him about!" I moaned turning over and covering my head with my pillow.

She grabbed the pillow and threw it and my quilt in a heap on the floor.

"If you decide you don't like him, okay, but at least get to know him. Now get up," she pulled on my arm again. "You have to work this afternoon anyway, don't you?"

I managed a nod and sat up. She wasn't going away.

"Isn't he cute?" she asked with a big grin. She backed a couple of steps away so I could get out of bed.

I mumbled something just to get her out of my hair.

"If he was a little older I'd be after him myself," she declared. She turned and strode back to her apartment.

I peeked around my door into the hallway to see if I could make it to the bathroom without being seen. I didn't own a housecoat. I threw a blanket around my shoulders and prayed I'd make it, grabbing some clothes to put on as I passed my closet.

I took a quick bath, slapped on some makeup, and then combed my hair. I put on my black pedal pushers and my clean white uniform blouse that I'd be wearing to work that day. We didn't have laundry facilities in the house. We had to walk to the Washateria down the street a couple of times a week because we could only carry a couple of small bundles of clothes. Our trip was a day or two overdue. But I took a last look in the mirror and decided I looked passable.

I smoothed my dark blondish hair. I had learned just recently how to "tease" it which made it more poufy—big hair was the new rage. I knew I had nice eyes, everybody commented about the fact that they changed from blue to green to gray depending on the colors I wore, and I got lots of compliments on my smile. I wiped a smudge of black liquid eye liner from the corner of one eye and took a deep breath. Either he'd like me or he wouldn't. I squared my shoulders and headed into Aggie's. I was learning every day how to put on a tough, I don't care attitude.

EVERMAN DRIVE

After breakfast and visiting for a while, I changed into my full uniform and James rode the bus with me back to Walnut Hill, walked me to Rocky's for my shift, and asked if he could see me again. I'd learned quite a bit about him that morning, he was eighteen, lived with his mom, and had dropped out of school. I didn't ask why. I just assumed his story was similar to mine and most kids I knew at the time. The main thing I learned was that I DID like him. And yes, I did want to see him again . . . and again!

From that day on he came in on my shift at least three or four days a week and would sit and keep me company while I ate lunch. On my days off he'd ride the bus to my house and spend the days with me and the nights on Aggie's couch. We never went anywhere; none of us could afford it. We didn't have a television so we listened to the radio and did a lot of kissing—so much so that our lips would get puffy and we'd have to take some time off to recover.

Yes, I'd learned how to kiss, long before I met James! I don't think there could have been anything more motivating than to be called tight lips by someone I idolized! So, I worked hard on it and never had another complaint!

Shortly after William had called me tight lips, I will never forget my Everman friend, Ruth Carol, telling me—maybe her sister Peanie and another neighborhood girl or two—that we should make SURE we never allowed a boy to "French kiss" us. I had never heard of that so I had to ask what it was.

Ruth Carol explained it was when a boy kissed you and stuck his tongue in your mouth.

"Ewwwww! Why would he do that," one of us asked, (maybe me, because I was desperate to learn how to do it right?).

I can't remember her exact words and she didn't go into detail but did explain that that was an extreme example of disrespect. She further said we wanted to make sure we acted at all times like ladies so that we wouldn't get bad reputations. That was Ruth Carol, ALWAYS looking out for the younger girls on Everman. We looked up to and listened to her. There were times in the next year or two that some date would try to French kiss me and I'd cut them off immediately. My reputation was very important to me and I'd gotten a lot of good role modeling and support in that area of life from my Everman friends.

So although James and I kissed until our lips swelled up and we had to take a break, he never tried to French kiss me and we never "went all the way". I knew better than that. Even my Celeste and Kingston friends whispered about that subject. We knew if you did that guys spread rumors and nobody would ever want you. The popular saying back then was, "if they can get the milk free, why buy the cow?"

Plus, I had living proof of what happens right on the second floor of my house. All I had to do was look at Aggie—she had a little kid she struggled constantly to take care of all by herself! In addition, when I was little my mother had pounded into my head that Jesus was watching me every minute and that (having sex out of marriage) was one of the worst sins, besides murder and blasphemy, that you could commit!

We hadn't gone to church in years but I hadn't forgotten that. I was determined to stay a virgin but it was difficult. When James was at my house, everyone was usually asleep or at work and my brothers were out somewhere. Besides, I LONGED for someone to love me and James was a very nice someone! And he didn't press me.

Just before Christmas I made a huge decision. I didn't like working at Rockyfeller's. The other employees were all older with families, the customers were older, especially the ones at the stand near Sunset High School—the tips were terrible and the extra forty cents an hour I made didn't come anywhere near to making up for the tips I was losing! Besides, I missed my friends at the Dairy Queen and the fun I always had with them as well as the teenage customers. I decided if Junior would have me I would go back.

James tried to talk me out of it.

"It's so far away we'll never get to see each other," he reasoned. "You'll be working weekends till all hours of the morning and you've even said you'll have to hitch rides home with . . . who knows who?"

I'm sure that was his main concern. He was worried about me getting rides home with other guys. But I'd made up my mind. I couldn't take another day working at Walnut Hill with that grumpy, old geezer, AL!

"I'll be okay," I assured James. "And we'll see each other."

I did like James a lot, maybe even loved him, but I was getting bored doing nothing but working and staying home. I wanted to be back out with my girlfriends, laughing, meeting new people, going for a coke after work. There HAD to be something besides work, home and worry!

Junior took me back immediately and I didn't even give a notice to Rockyfeller's which didn't make my mother happy, but then nothing did! It was wonderful being back at D. Q. My coworkers and the regular customers were happy to see me although most couldn't resist an "I told you so!"

By this time Billie had been in beauty school for a couple of months and she needed a model to practice a bleach job on. She asked me what I thought about it. She said she could make me look like Marilyn Monroe or Sandra Dee. All I had to do was buy the bleach and toner. So I jumped at the chance. She told me what to buy, I did, and she spent the night in my room one night and transformed me the next morning. I loved the results. Everybody I knew commented on the change. Many liked it, some didn't. I didn't care. I did feel like a movie star. But I was so ignorant, I didn't know before I did it, that you had to touch up the roots about every month or so. My "do" was so pale blonde it only took a couple of weeks for my natural color—even though it wasn't that dark—to start showing.

James was one who didn't like it. He saw it the week after Billie bleached it.

He was shocked, I could tell, but all he said was, "I like your hair better the other way."

I hadn't expected that response from him but I could tell that he was still upset that I'd changed jobs. I think he'd maybe unconsciously taken that as an indication that I didn't want to see him as often. That visit wasn't that comfortable or fun.

In the meantime I was having to get most of my rides home with Raina and Junie and their Redtop beer. We indulged a couple times a week.

One night about three weeks after Billie did my hair, she, the two sisters, Zana, and I went out after work. Billie and Zana got dropped off early and the sisters and I bought some Redtop. I drank way too much. When they let me out of the car I fell several times before getting to my front steps. They sped off leaving me to make my way up the stairs. I was trying to be quiet because it was at least two in the morning but I was having problems with the stairs. I gave up halfway to the landing and began crawling on all fours. Just as I reached the halfway mark I heard a male voice say, "You look like a drunken slut!"

I looked up and James was standing at the top of the landing, hands on hips.

I stopped in shock, as drunk as I was, that he would talk to me like that. Then I burst into tears.

He walked down and helped me to my feet and half carried me into my room, all the while yelling at me for drinking.

"Don't you care about yourself? Only sluts act like this."

He was furious.

I cried harder.

He disappeared into the bathroom, retrieved a warm wet wash cloth and began to wash my face and try to get my hair to do something besides stick straight up.

"I'm sorry; I don't mean to be so hard on you, Linda. Don't cry," he soothed, putting his arms around me, kissing my forehead, my cheek and then my lips.

"I'm sorry I yelled at you."

I put my arms around his neck and clung to him. I had missed him and I was drunk. I just wanted to be held. He responded and we lay back across my bed, keeping our clothes on as usual. Oh, I loved to kiss, especially after a few drinks and we were really getting into it. I was so filled with the joy of seeing him and the fact that he had finally begun to show me how much he had missed me, that I couldn't contain myself.

I moaned, "Oh Billie . . ."

The minute it came out of my mouth I knew I'd made a huge mistake. I didn't even know why I said it except I was drunk.

He stiffened, pushed me away and said in a very low, menacing tone, "Who the hell is Billy?"

I tried to tell him it was one of my best girlfriends, the one who'd bleached my hair, but he wasn't buying it.

"Then why would you be calling her name?" he asked. "Tell me! Is Billy some guy you've been going out with?"

"No! The only Billie I know is the girl I work with. I don't know why I said her name! It just came out," I pleaded. "I meant to say James!"

But he wasn't convinced.

When I awoke mid-morning he was asleep beside me but as far away as he could get without falling off the double bed. I got up and stumbled to the bathroom. My head was pounding and I thought I was going to be sick. I washed my face and ran a comb through my hair trying to remember if we had any aspirin in the apartment. I couldn't think, and knew I wouldn't make it to the corner store. I leaned down and drank cold water straight from the faucet. When I got back to my room James was awake and sitting on the end of the bed. He shook his head in disgust. I slid back into bed and covered my head with the blanket. I was miserable. I'd never had a headache this bad.

"How could you do this?" James asked softly.

I didn't answer.

"Who were you with last night?" he persisted. "How did you get the booze?"

"I was with the girls I work with," I said. "They bought it."

I uncovered my head and peeked out at him. I knew I looked horrible but not as bad as I felt.

"Don't you care what people think of you?" he demanded.

I nodded my head and felt dizzy.

"Then will you stop drinking? You're going to get yourself in trouble."

I nodded again, very slowly this time, so the room would stay still. I was ashamed. Probably more so because he'd seen me looking like this.

"And this 'Billy' thing . . . ." He raked his fingers through his hair. "I don't know whether to believe you or not."

All of a sudden the slip of my tongue came back to me. Then anger flared.

"Have I lied to you before?" I demanded.

"I don't know, have you?"

"No I haven't! So why would I start now?" I said, so loud my head pounded.

"I don't know. Sometimes I feel like you're just using me," he said.

That floored me and ticked me off more. I laughed out loud. He shouldn't have said that!

"Using you for what, for heaven's sake? For your money? Your car? All the fancy places you take me?"

I was on a roll. It was a matter of pride that I could take care of myself!

His face turned red and his eyes lost their sparkle. I knew I'd hurt him, but I wouldn't back down. He had no right telling me what to do. What I'd said was true. We'd never even been to a movie! Mama said if a guy really loved you he wouldn't let you go through hard times by yourself. And at that young age, even though I didn't trust her in many things, I still thought she knew more about men and how they were. It would take me years to back away from ANYTHING she said!

"Maybe I shouldn't come back until I have money and a car then!" he offered.

"Maybe you shouldn't," I yelled as loud as my headache would allow. I was very angry. He wasn't going to accuse me of using him!

He turned and headed for the door.

"Okay. I'll see you then." He walked out and down the stairs.

I thought sure he'd be back in a little while. After two weeks I gave up. I realized I'd gone too far. I'd hurt his pride. I was sad and missed him, but there wasn't a lot of time to dwell on it. I was working double shifts. The boys who came in to the drive-in were constantly flirting and asking me out. That soothed my pride somewhat. James wasn't the only fish in the sea, I told myself. Plus, I was hanging out with the sisters, and Billie—when she had free time, and there were problems to attend to at home.

Christmas day 1962 dawned and it was a day that no kid should ever have had to face! The Dairy Queen was closed. Rockyfeller's was open so Mama worked but Aggie was off. It was cold and gray looking outside and nothing to do inside. We had no food, no tree, no decorations, and no presents. It seemed as if nobody cared if we lived or died. Daddy hadn't even sent a

Christmas card. That wasn't a big surprise. If it involved money, even a dollar or two, he was nowhere to be found.

Before their divorce Mama had always made sure we at least had a tree even if she had to be the one to tromp into the woods to cut it down. She showed us how to make paste out of flour and water and we'd cut strips from construction paper and paste them into a garland to wrap around the tree. Then we'd pop corn and use a sewing needle and thread to string a long chain to wind around the tree. A time or two she'd snuck some tinsel into her shopping basket at the grocery store when Daddy wasn't looking. We thought those "ice cycles" were the prettiest things. We put them on the tree separately to make sure they were spread evenly. When the time came to get rid of the tree we'd take the ice cycles off, one at a time, and use them the next several Christmas' until they finally fell apart in our hands.

And she'd make sure we had at least one present, even if she had to make it. But, she'd ruin Christmas because we'd start asking for hints about our gifts and she couldn't keep a secret. So she'd break them out of their hiding places days or weeks before Christmas, and give them to us. We liked that for a few days but then the only thing we had to look forward to on the big day was a little better dinner than normal—usually fried chicken (that she'd picked out of our small flock early that morning and wrung it's neck), mashed potatoes, gravy, green peas and biscuits or cornbread. If we were lucky she'd whip up a cake or pie. If money was extra tight she'd fry up individual chocolate pies in her old black iron skillet using biscuit dough, Hershey's cocoa, sugar and a little fresh cow's milk. You could say getting the gifts too early was our fault, but we were kids—I was only about five to eight years old, my brothers much younger. You'd think she would be strong enough to withhold the gifts until Christmas.

We never had company on holidays or any other time. My parents didn't have friends. Neither did I until I started school. A few times we did barge in on my mother's aunt Vera and Uncle Jesse who lived in Sulphur Springs on holidays and it strikes me now that we never took any food to contribute. We ate well though! Aunt Vera was a phenomenal cook and would have several different meats, vegetables, sweets, and everyone who showed up got their fill. Of course, after I started school I'd hear from friends how their holidays went, how many presents they got, etc., and I'd dream someday I would experience holidays like that.

But as bad as my early Christmas' had been, NONE had ever been as horrible as that one in 1962. Aggie was having a terrible time as well. She'd had to miss a couple days work earlier in the week so her check was short. After putting aside her rent, she had managed to buy Andy a cheap toy and a few jars of baby food, but her refrigerator was just as empty as ours.

She and I finally bundled up the baby and our dirty laundry and lugged them to the local Washateria which was open twenty-four hours a day, seven days a week. My brothers stayed home because of the cold. We were the only ones washing that Christmas day which didn't surprise either of us. We sat in the plastic chairs by the front window and stared out at the decorations on houses and store fronts. We made up stories about the celebrations we were going to have someday.

We were both so depressed by the time we finished the clothes that we decided to spend the rest of the change we had to buy ourselves and the boys a Rockyfeller hamburger for supper.

We dropped the clothes at the apartment and walked to the Rocky's on Jefferson near Sunset High. Rocky's burgers were nothing more than two small buns, a thin slice of hamburger meat, minced onions, and a ketchup-based sauce called Rocky's Special Sauce. They cost twenty cents each and we just barely had enough to buy two apiece. Aggie had some R. C. cola and that was a blessing or else we would have had to wash our burgers down with water.

Frankie and Gary devoured theirs like they hadn't eaten for days. It's quite possible they hadn't. There was never any food in the apartment. I wasn't sure if that was because the boys kept everything eaten up or because there was nothing there to begin with. Even though we were very hungry Aggie and I had eaten so many hamburgers while working at Rockefeller's that we had to force down the last few bites. I kept thinking of all those people out there who were going to be complaining about eating leftovers tomorrow. We would have, right then, gratefully scrubbed somebody's floors and toilets for left-over's of any kind!

I couldn't understand why we were always in such dire straits.

"Aggie, do you know anything about God?"

"I don't even know if there is one!" she answered.

"Well when I was little and went to Sunday school they used to tell us all the time how much God loves His children. If that's true, how can He just forget about us? Aren't we His children too? How come some people have so much and we have nothing?"

"Beats me. But I'll tell you one thing," she had tears in her eyes when she looked up at me. "I don't care what I have to do; I ain't going through another Christmas like this!"

We sat around her apartment for a while longer trying to cheer each other up. Finally, I went to my room and turned on my radio. My brothers drifted in a few minutes later and lay down across the foot of my bed. Neither of them said anything. I could tell they were depressed too. I didn't know what to say to them. We listened silently to the Christmas carols and they ended up falling asleep. I didn't have the heart to wake and send them into the empty apartment. I crawled in at my end and slept fitfully until morning. My dream was about Mama. In it, she didn't look or act like anyone I knew. I kept trying to find out what had happened to her. Why had she changed so much? But when she opened her mouth to explain nothing came out but the sound of the wind.

I awoke close to noon the next day, drug myself out of bed and started getting ready for work. Frankie and Gary were already gone, the apartment empty. I didn't have to be at work until five but I was spending a lot of my free time there, hanging around to talk to anyone who had time for me. If they got busy I'd pitch in and help for nothing. Or, I'd just sit, smoke and drink coffee. Refills were free and almost anything was better than going home.

That night when the D. Q. closed I had no place else except home to go to. By then everyone was asleep.

Chapter Nine

The next morning Aggie knocked on my door before leaving for her shift. Andy was on one hip and a big box wrapped in Christmas paper on the other. I thought she was taking it with her to give to someone, maybe Andy's babysitter who did a lot of overtime sitting. But when I got my eyes completely open and my brain going I realized she was handing the box to me.

"Oh Aggie! You don't have the money for this!"

I felt terrible! I had nothing for her.

"It's not from me," she grinned, eyes sparkling. "Open it!"

I was so stunned I couldn't move. I just stood there with it in my hands, my mouth hanging open. Aggie's smile was the biggest I'd seen on her face for a long while.

"Santa Claus remembered you after all, that's a good sign," she said,

"Who's it from?" I demanded.

She shook her head.

"Quit talking and open it!"

I ripped the paper in nothing flat and tore off the top. Inside was the most beautiful beige two-piece suit with a gorgeous fake fur attached to the collar by snaps. I gasped. I'd never owned anything this nice. Aggie oohed and aahed right along with me.

I jerked it out of the box and ran to the mirror in the bathroom with Aggie right behind. I held it up against me. It was the right size and I could tell already it was going to look great. I turned to Aggie.

"Who got it for me?"

I still couldn't believe it. I was afraid any minute she was going to take it back and say it was all a joke but her eyes were shining.

"It's from James," she said.

I was stunned.

"He was going to send it to you Christmas day but he didn't know I had the day off. He had to wait until I came back yesterday. He got your Mama and me a present too. Wait 'til you see them."

"What did he get Mama?"

"One of those new portable hair dryers. Boy, I'd like to have one of those!"

"What did you get?"

"I got a beautiful blouse and a pair of matching earrings."

I was glad she got something too, but since he got all three of us something it kind of took some of the specialness away. I forced that thought out of my mind. *How selfish could I get?*

"Why'd he do this? I haven't heard from him in a couple of weeks. I thought he'd forgotten all about me."

I started back to my room and grabbed a hanger from my closet. Aggie had trailed along behind. I arranged the suit on the hanger.

"Oh, he's been in just about every night. He asks about you, what you're doing, what's going on, all that stuff," she said.

"How come he just doesn't come see for himself?" I asked.

"Well, I think he feels you don't want anything to do with him. Maybe he's been waiting to see if you would get in touch with him? I don't know. I know he misses you though. Why don't you call him?"

"I don't know his phone number," I said.

Besides wouldn't that count as "chasing a boy"? I can't do that!

I looked back at the suit hanging in my closet. I did miss him but didn't know if it was because he was the only person I could count on. I knew he liked me a lot, maybe even loved me but he wanted me to be his girl only. And while that sounded safe and secure I was only fifteen years old and wanted to see things, do things, and be somebody someday. I didn't want to be tied down just yet. He wouldn't understand that. He would take it as a rejection of him.

"I can't call him, Aggie. Tell him that I love my present and I'm sorry I don't have anything for him. Tell him I would like for him to come by . . . I'd like to see him."

I hoped he would know I meant it.

I looked at Aggie, hoping she'd know how to get that across to him.

She shrugged.

"Okay. I hope you know what you're doing. He's a great guy."

I had to wipe away tears. I hoped I wasn't making a mistake. But how would I know? I sure didn't have anyone I could go to for guidance. And though I like Aggie a lot, she hadn't done such a good job with the choices she'd made so far.

After Aggie left for work I tried the suit on and had never looked so good. The only place I could think of to go dressed up like that was the downtown stores like Niemen Marcus. I'd walked past those fancy stores every day when changing busses to go to the Walnut Hill Rocky's. All the shoppers who went in through their doors were dressed to their teeth, suits, high heels, hats. I couldn't go inside because I was always in my cheap waitress uniform. But I'd wanted to. Just to see how the other half lived. I didn't ride the bus to Walnut Hill anymore and had no reason to go up town.

I turned to one side to admire myself from that angle. I reached up and fluffed my bangs. I would have to do something with my hair. I now had a lot of out-growth. I couldn't afford to go to a beauty shop, and Billie was too busy to do anything right now.

I sighed. *Someday* . . . .

January was a cold dreary month. I had my new coat to keep me warm but Mama had taken all the joy out of wearing it. Every time I put it on I remembered the accusation she'd yelled at me. Neither one of us had ever spoken of it. I hardly ever saw her. I saw Aggie a lot more.

It was Aggie that told me Mama had been notified by the boys' school that Frankie had been missing a lot since November. He'd turned in notes allegedly signed by Mama but of course he'd forged them.

Aggie said Mama had no idea where Frankie had been staying during the day and he wasn't telling. After a half-hearted warning Mama resumed ignoring the situation.

Aggie also added that Frankie and Gary had been fighting a lot. She'd had to intervene in several knock-down-drag-outs. Frankie was bullying Gary, and Gary was too little to defend himself. Aggie said the whole situation was bad. They needed somebody to rein them in.

I admit I forgot about it too. James had come back over to see me the week after I received his Christmas gift and he'd been riding the bus over once a week on my days off since then. He continued to spend the nights at Aggie's and we spent the days just hanging out in the apartment or my room listening to my radio.

Two weeks after Aggie had filled me in on Frankie's bullying Gary I witnessed the aftermath of one of the brawls she had described. I came in from work early—there hadn't been enough customers to keep two carhops busy. Since I had already worked seven days straight, some of those double shifts, Junior told me to go home. I was upset. I didn't know why it mattered; we didn't get paid overtime, so it was no skin off Junior's nose if I worked around the clock for the rest of my life! I didn't want to go home but a guy I knew came in and offered me a ride. I accepted.

When I got out of the car I could hear my brothers yelling at each other. As I started up the stairs Frankie came rolling down them, head over heels, howling. He almost knocked me down before he came to rest against the wall at the first landing. He had a death grip on a slice of white bread folded around a piece of bologna. When he stood up I saw blood on the back of his T shirt. I looked up at the top of the stairs where Gary was standing holding a fork, sobbing hysterically.

"He took my sandwich!" Gary screamed.

I looked at Frankie who was trying with one hand to reach the spot on his back where the blood was spotting his grimy T shirt. He was half laughing, half crying.

"What's going on?" I demanded, grabbing Frankie and turning him around to look at his back. There were four little puncture holes between his shoulder blades, not life threatening by any means but deep enough to hurt. The holes had been put there by the fork.

"I didn't think he had the guts!" Frankie laughed, staring at Gary trying to pretend he didn't have tears in his eyes.

I grabbed the sandwich from his hand. He looked startled.

"Is this Gary's?" I demanded.

"Yesssssss!" Gary screamed. "He already ate his and then he stole mine and there ain't anymore!"

"Okay, then you can have it back. Frankie you better leave him alone. I mean it!"

I went up the stairs two at a time and handed the food to Gary. He was still sobbing. I put my arm around him and guided him into my room, shutting and locking the door. I had him sit on my bed. I sat beside him putting my arms around him, trying to calm him down.

Frankie stood out in the hall pounding on my door.

I ignored the noise.

"What's going on?" I asked Gary.

"Frankie's always picking on me! He hits me, he hogs all the food . . . one of these days I'm going to kill him!" Gary sobbed

From the other side of the door Frankie yelled, "Yeah you big baby! You ain't gonna do nothing!"

I put my arm around Gary and said softly, "You can't even think stuff like that Gary. It's okay, even good, to take up for yourself, but you can't use forks or knives and things like that. You're gonna get yourself in trouble, maybe hurt somebody bad. Have you told Mama how he treats you?"

"She won't do nothing but tell him to leave me alone and then when nobody's here he just picks on me for fun!" He was still sobbing. The tears were mixing with the dirt on his face and making trails down his cheeks.

"Well I'll tell her this time. Go ahead and eat your sandwich. You can stay in here with me tonight."

I smoothed the hair back from his forehead. It was too long and needed a good shampooing. They didn't get haircuts often, we couldn't afford it.

Frankie was still at the door listening and hit the door three more times then yelled, "He can stay in there with you, I don't care! He ain't nothin' but a big cry baby, anyway!" He kicked the door for good measure and then stomped away singing, "Cry baby, cry baby."

Gary was still amped up. He yelled, "Shut up, stupid!"

I grabbed Gary's arm and said, "Just ignore him. Eat your sandwich."

"Cry baby . . . ," sang Frankie, and then we heard the door to the apartment slam shut.

I turned on my radio and soon Gary was calm enough to eat. I had him lie down at the foot of my bed and it wasn't long before he fell asleep. I would make it a point in the morning to fill Mama in, but knew Gary was right. She'd tell Frankie to behave himself and then go to work and forget it.

Frankie had been bullying kids for years, all the way back to that summer I'd been locked up with baby Karen and the Mexican girls had tried to take him to task for it. He'd go right back to doing what he darn well pleased. Why shouldn't he? Nobody cared except the kid getting bullied. I made up my mind to try to watch them more closely when I was home to see that Gary was not Frankie's go-to punching bag.

I worked every day for the next several days and didn't see Mama or Aggie. Once or twice I intervened in a scuffle between the boys and threatened to beat the stuffing out of Frankie if he didn't leave Gary alone. But he'd gotten so big nothing I said made a difference. He wasn't afraid of me unless I grabbed the broom or something similar to threaten him with. I'm sure though when I wasn't home Gary paid for it. When I finally saw Mama and told her what was going on, she did what she usually did . . . nothing!

What could or should she have done? I didn't know then and don't know now! She had to work the hours she did just to keep a roof over our head. She had no support (partly her fault!) and hadn't had for years. We had no money for baby sitters. All the choices she and my father had made in the past—most of them bad—had led to the way we were living at that time. It was probably, by then, too late to change the directions my brothers were taking—experts say our personalities are formed at a very young age. But it could have made a difference. It would have been nice if SOMEBODY had tried!

Toward the latter part of January James and I had a silly argument. I can't even remember what it was about. He was at my house, he'd ridden the bus over to see me on my day off, but I was in one of my depressed moods and felt the walls closing in on me. I didn't want to be penned up in the apartment my two days off. Neither one of us had any money to go anywhere. I wanted to go out to the D. Q. and hang out with Billie and Zana. I paced the floors, I was up-tight and antsy, and of course, James could tell I was bored. I'm sure he felt terrible.

He hung around for a while but then decided to go home a day early. I didn't try to stop him.

As he walked out the door he said, "I think you don't really care as much about me as I do for you."

I didn't know what to say. He just looked at me for a moment, said "bye" and then turned and left. I felt terrible. I wanted to run after him and say I'm sorry but didn't. I went back in my room and collapsed into tears, more out of anger and frustration at the life I was living than anything else.

I continued to work, come home, sleep, go to work, come home, sleep. I didn't hear from James.

The last week of January Aggie woke me to let me know James had been shot and was in the Parkland hospital in critical condition. She wasn't sure how it had happened. She had spoken with his mother via phone the night before who said it was a bullet to the stomach, and she didn't know how it happened. Aggie didn't know if they were allowing visitors outside of family but she was going by Parkland Hospital on her way to work to find out.

I was in shock.

"Somebody shot him?"

"No, from what I understand, he was cleaning a gun and it went off. His mom was in no condition to talk. She said he'd asked her to call me," Aggie said.

"Well, is he okay?"

What I meant was *is he going to live?* I was afraid to put that into words.

"I'll know more when I get to the hospital. If I get to see him, do you want me to tell him anything?" she asked.

My brain was spinning, nothing was making sense.

What could I say to him? *Get well soon . . . I hope you feel better . . . ?* Neither seemed appropriate.

I hadn't known anyone who'd ever been hospitalized, much less shot! And this was James! What could I say?

"Tell him I'm sorry."

I knew by Aggie's expression she'd hoped I had something to say that was a little deeper than that.

I shrugged.

"I don't know what to say," I admitted.

"Do you want to go see him?"

"Yes, but I don't have a way," I answered. "And I have to work tonight."

"Let me find out what's going on and I'll get us a ride there as soon as I find out about visitors," she promised as she waved goodbye and headed for the stairs. "I have an idea that's the main reason he told his mom to call me. He knew I'd tell you."

I heard the lower door slam and silence settled over the house again.

I lay back down and stared at the ceiling. I kept remembering how the light had gone out of his eyes the last time I saw him.

How could this happen? Was he going to die?

When I got home that night I found a note on my door:

If everything goes okay between now and then, James can have visitors tomorrow. I got us a ride. See me in the morning.

The next morning I learned that one of Aggie's customers had agreed to take us to the hospital. Her friend, Ernie, was in his mid-forties and had been interested in Aggie for a while. I'd seen him a couple of times when Aggie and I had worked together. He was nice but a plain looking blah kind of guy.

We were going in the evening so I walked to the store on the corner and used the pay phone to make arrangements with Billie to take over my shift. I was worried about James. And worried about what I'd say to him.

When Aggie's friend picked us up Mama was there and decided to go as well. The three of them rode in the front seat. I was alone in the back. Aggie filled her friend in on who we were going to see, how we knew him, and what had happened. I listened intently because I still didn't know the details.

"Was it his gun?" Ernie asked.

"I'm assuming it was. His mother said he told her he was cleaning it when it went off," Aggie responded.

"I don't believe it," Mama said. How many people do you know who try to clean a gun when it's loaded?"

"He may not have known it was loaded,"

Mama cut her off. "James isn't stupid!"

I leaned forward to hear better.

Aggie turned and stared at Mama.

"You think it wasn't an accident?" Aggie asked staring at Mama, a look of surprise on her face.

"You know how he's been lately!"

My stomach lurched. Aggie looked straight ahead and said nothing.

Mama continued, "He's been so depressed over Linda, maybe he decided to do it to either end it all . . . or to get her attention."

I felt like the breath had been knocked out of me. I'd never considered that possibility.

Oh man! Could that be true? Could it be my fault?

I struggled to catch my breath. No one in the front seat paid any attention to me.

Guilt washed over me in waves.

I should have done something, talked to him, apologized, seen him . . . But how could I have known?

I was shaking. If I was the cause how was I going to face him? I looked around wildly. If only I could think of a way to escape. But then if Mama was right and I didn't respond, would he try to do something else to himself?

Aggie and her friend changed the subject. Every once in a while Mama joined in the conversation. I wasn't listening. I was reliving everything I'd said and done the last time I'd seen him. Yes, I'd been too hard on him. He'd given me that beautiful

Christmas gift and I knew it had cost him a pretty penny. I hadn't even worn it for him yet—but all we did was stay home!

My stomach was rolling. I wished I'd never heard this stuff. I didn't know what to do. I hoped his mother wasn't there when we arrived. She'd probably think it was my fault too and I'd never even met her. I didn't know how I could face him! I was so nervous I thought I was going to be sick. Aggie, Ernie, and Mama walked ahead. I followed. The closer we got to his room the more I panicked. I forced myself to enter behind the other three. And what I saw made me feel even worse.

James lay in the bed with tubes running into his nose and his arm. He was almost as white as the sheet that covered him to his waist. A huge white bandage ran completely across his stomach clear up to the middle of his chest. He looked thin and drawn. And when he responded to Aggie's "hi", his voice was low and cracked, like that of an old man. Aggie and Mama gathered close to his bedside. Ernie hung back a few steps after he was introduced.

I stopped at the foot of his bed and swallowed hard. His eyes found me and bored into mine. Mama was saying something to him but I didn't catch it. I wasn't sure he even heard her because he didn't respond.

"Hi," I said and then felt completely stupid. I'd never even been inside a hospital before. *What do you say to someone in this condition?*

"Hi," he answered still staring into my eyes. He looked so sad. I was immediately hit with another round of guilt. Even those beautiful eyes looked dead.

Everyone was watching me. I swallowed again and walked around to the other side of the bed to get closer to him.

"How are you?" I asked.

He tried to smile.

"Well, I've been better...."

He slowly reached his hand out to me. I took it and held it gently. I was afraid I'd hurt him. Out of the corner of my eye I could see the others staring. I felt in a way, that I was on some kind of stage and they were judging my performance. I didn't know what else to say. I hadn't seen James since our argument so it wasn't like we could pick right up from where we left off.

Mama filled the silence.

"How long you gonna be in the hospital James?"

I released his hand and he turned his head slowly to look at her as he answered.

"They haven't told me yet," he said.

He looked back at me. There were too many people watching . . . we couldn't talk so we didn't. I mostly stared everywhere except at him but I could see him watching me, except when he responded to questions from Aggie and Mama. I was horribly uncomfortable. Finally, Aggie said we had to go. We said our goodbyes and gave him hugs. The last thing I saw when I walked out the door was those beautiful brown eyes, huge and sad, his pale thin face. I raised my hand and he gave me a slight wave as well.

I told myself I'd find a way to go back and talk to him. I wanted to find out the truth about the gunshot, and try to explain my feelings. But I was extremely relieved to be getting out of there. Having the power of life and death over another person was too much for me. I wanted to get away from that responsibility as soon as possible.

And though I thought a lot about James over the next several days that was exactly what I came back to: that it probably was my fault he'd almost died. So, in order to handle the guilt and shame I did my best not to think of him at all. I'd think about it later.

Getting my new Hi Fi out of layaway helped tremendously. I even splurged and bought one of my favorite 45 records; Englebert Humperdinck's *Release Me*. But, I must admit every time I heard those words I thought of James. I liked him a lot, but didn't want to have to be afraid all the time that I'd do something to make him try to hurt himself. I wasn't convinced that that's what had happened, but didn't know for sure, and that was a heavy burden to bear.

A few days later I came home to find Aggie and Andy gone. When I reached the second floor landing her door stood open so I poked my head in and you-hoo'd. The furniture was still there of course, because the apartments were furnished, but everything else had been stripped. I was shocked and numb.

What happened? How could she just leave and not say goodbye?!

Something had happened. I immediately suspected my mother. I waited until she came home and asked if they'd gotten into a fight. She refused to talk about it. All I got was "you tend to your business and I'll tend to mine!"

Aggie was the closest friend I had and now she was just gone. The upper floor was so deserted it echoed. But I didn't cry.

During the first part of February Mama came down with the Asian flu. Within two days the boys got it as well. Mama was out of her head with fever. Without her pay and daily tips we ran out of food quickly.

By the time I started to feel sick Mama had begun to rally. She told me to go to a pay phone and call my father to see if he would loan us ten dollars until we could get back on our feet. I didn't want to ask him but the boys needed milk, soup, maybe some 7-up. We had nothing.

I trudged down to the corner phone booth dreading it all the way. I tried rehearsing my speech because Daddy didn't part with his money easily. I hadn't seen him in a long time.

I smoked a Winston and then put a dime in the phone and asked the operator to help me with a collect call. That was the first hurdle. He'd refused a collect call from me once before. I held my breath while the operator told him who was calling and then waited while he took a few moments to decide if he wanted to accept or not.

"Sir . . . ?" the operator prompted.

"Well, I guess . . . this one time," he warned.

"Hi Daddy," I said, feeling like a beggar.

"Hi," was all he said.

"Daddy, Mama's been real sick with the flu and can't work and Frankie and Gary are sick too. We don't have anything to eat. I'm feeling like I'm coming down with it. Could you loan us ten dollars for a couple of weeks so I can buy some milk, bread, and stuff?"

I could feel my words tumbling over each other to try to get everything out before he could answer.

Another silent pause.

"Naw, I can't," he said. "I've still got to buy feed for my cows and horses for the rest of the winter."

"I'll pay you back, Daddy. We don't have anything to eat!" I pleaded.

"That damned ol' heifer should have thought of that before she dragged you kids away from me!" he exploded. "If it hadn't been for her you'd be here and have plenty to eat," he finished. An absolute lie, unless he meant plenty of peanut butter!

"Then you can't?" I couldn't say the word *won't*, but I knew that was the right word. I had a huge lump in my throat. He wasn't rich by any means but he and I both knew he could loan me ten or fifteen dollars and still take care of his animals. It was apparent his own kids weren't as important as his cows!

"Naw. I don't see how I can," he insisted. "But you can come back here and live."

"Okay, then. I'll see ya."

I hung up before he could say anything else and made a promise right then and there: *I'd NEVER ask him for another thing!*

Chapter Ten

When I got home I told Mama what Daddy had said. She was silent for a minute then she got up and started dressing to go out. She didn't look good and seemed sort of woozy. Frankie and Gary were asleep at the foot of her bed. She reached over and covered them with a quilt. Gary stirred but didn't wake up. She touched the back of her hand to their foreheads, checking their fever, but didn't say anything.

"Where are you going?" I asked.

I saw the grim, determined look on her face.

"To get us something to eat," she said.

"Where?" I asked.

"I don't know. You just remember how that sorry so and so felt about y'all! He doesn't even care if you starve to death!" she fumed.

I knew it already but it hurt more when she spoke it out loud. I walked into the front room and sank onto the couch.

"Keep your eye on the boys. I won't be gone long."

She tied a scarf around her head, grabbed her coat and stormed out the front door.

I stretched out on the couch. I felt awful!

Two hours later she was back with two small bags of groceries. She'd even managed to get Bayer aspirin for fever.

"Where'd you get this?" I asked. I didn't feel like eating but was glad there would be something for later.

"There's a preacher who's been coming into Rocky's and he told me once if there was anything I needed to give him a call. He loaned me a few dollars until I can get another check." She began putting the food into the tiny refrigerator.

I took two aspirin and curled up on the sofa. When I awoke a little later my fever was way up. I took a couple drinks of orange juice and then returned to the couch. I must have been out of my head with fever for the next twenty-four hours because I don't remember a thing.

I returned to work before I should have, we needed the money so badly. It was hard to get back into the swing of things because I felt so weak.

Within a few days I was back to my old self. Mama noticed and commented. I was surprised. It had been a long time since she'd payed any attention to any of us.

"How would you like to go to California for a vacation?" she asked casually as she stared into a mirror applying Pond's face cream.

I was stunned. *How could we manage a vacation to anywhere?* We'd just had to borrow money to eat?!

"California?" I stuttered.

"Mama Davis and Paw Paw will pay for a train ticket for all of us. We'll have to pay it back later but think about this. We haven't seen them since you were little. We can stay with them for free, rest and visit a little, maybe visit Yosemite, Hollywood, see what the ocean looks like? It would be fun. We haven't ever had a real vacation. We could come back rested and with a whole different attitude. What do you think?"

She made small, gentle circles with the face cream until her face and neck shined with the stuff.

I stared at her and thought about the possibilities. I vaguely remembered my grandparents. We'd made a car trip to visit them when I was in the first grade and of course I'd seen them when we went to Arizona to pick Pima cotton when I was in the second grade. They'd been in California since 1950 because they worked in the fruit and vegetable crops. But, I was afraid of my grandfather. I saw him whip his children and grandchildren who were close to my age with a razor strap. I'd tip-toed around him both visits but Daddy kept telling me not to worry the "old man" would lay a hand on me over his dead body!

My overwhelming thought was the idea of getting to go to Hollywood and seeing movie stars, Yosemite, and the ocean. I could "see" myself lying on the beach listening to the waves hit the shore. I'd need to get a bathing suit! I started getting excited but contained myself enough to ask some practical questions.

"How will we pay our rent? We won't be working."

"Well, you remember the Preacher who helped us when we were sick?"

"Yeah. Have you paid him back yet?"

"He's offered to store some of our stuff and we could let the apartment go and just find another one—maybe a better one—when we get back."

She was looking at me with something of a smile and excitement of her own.

"Lord knows it's about time we got some kind of break! Opportunities like this don't come along every day. I think we ought to jump at it!" she finished.

I was warming to the idea, seeing images in my mind of running in to Elvis, Elizabeth Taylor, Sandra Dee, and Marilyn Monroe.

Oh! I wouldn't care which star it was!

"When would we leave? How long would we be gone? I don't know if Junior would let me off work that long."

Then I flashed on a mental picture of me lying on a beach, slathered with Coppertone, talking to brown skinned, blonde-haired surfer guys like the Beach Boys. Their records, *Surfin' U.S.A.*, and *409* were all the rage at the D. Q.

That would be so groovy!

"I'm going to call Paw Paw again in a couple of days, and I'll let you know more after that." She went into the bathroom to get ready for work.

I was skeptical but continued to daydream. She seemed serious and had been around a lot longer than I had.

Maybe we could pull it off?

I started talking about it to my friends, even bragging a little. Billie was excited for me.

"Wow. I don't know if I'll ever get to do anything like that," she gushed. "If you see any movie stars, get me an autograph too, okay?"

I said I would.

She fingered my hair.

"You can't meet movie stars looking like this. Buy the bleach and stuff and I'll fix your hair. You can use my discount to buy everything," she said.

"All right! Thanks Billie."

It looked like I was finally running into some good luck.

Mama settled on March the third to leave. I talked to Junior. He agreed to hold my job for fifteen days—we were only supposed to be gone ten.

Then I told Doyle, a very nice guy I'd dated three or four times in the last couple of weeks. He was not happy.

"I don't know why you have to go there," he complained. "There ain't nothin' there but fruits and nuts!"

I heard that a lot from my customers but didn't ask for clarification.

My joy was dampened a few days later though when Mama said the only thing we could take with us was a few clothes. That meant I had to leave my radio, my Hi Fi, my stuffed dog, and my records with someone I'd never met. I'd managed to buy several 45's and one 78 rpm album. She assured me the Preacher and his family would take good care of everything.

A week before we left Billie touched up my roots. She said I looked like a movie star myself.

Finally, the day of departure arrived. Mama had picked up the two babies, Karen and Terry Lee. I hadn't been around the little ones in so long I almost didn't recognize them. They didn't know any of us. Terry Lee cried the whole time. He'd been with Dora, the baby sitter, since he was a tiny little thing and he was missing her. Imagine how scared those babies had to be with total strangers and their "Mama" missing? Karen tried to get away and inspect everything. Both were upset. They had no idea what was going on—they'd just been torn from their "Mama" Dora!

We were all bathed and in our best clothes. Mama had fried two chickens, and baked some biscuits. We each had one paper sack filled with our clothes—I had packed my sack tight! Her Preacher friend picked us up and loaded my precious belongings into his trunk—I wondered why Mama wasn't having him save anything of hers. But I didn't dwell on it because each time we'd moved we'd left stuff behind. He took us to the train station. I sat in the back seat with the kids.

As the train approached the Preacher shook Mama's hand and wished her good luck. I thought he was saying that because the kids were so noisy.

It took three days and two nights to get to Fresno. We all needed a bath, a change of clothes and a good night's sleep. Our food, even being rationed by Mama, played out on the second evening. On the third morning, she bought two hamburgers from the dining car and split them between all six of us. By the time we pulled into the depot in Fresno we were starving, the two babies were still crying, and Frankie and Gary were arguing.

It must have been obvious to the man running the desk inside the depot that we were down and out because he took one look at us and handed each one of us kids a candy bar. I was embarrassed. But not so much that I refused the candy.

By the time we gulped them down my grandfather, grandmother, and Rosemary one of my mother's sisters, arrived to pick us up. I was shocked at their appearance. They looked worse than the characters in the Ma and Pa Kettle movies I'd seen back in Greenville.

My grandfather's bushy black hair looked like it hadn't been combed in days. He breathed through his mouth and every once in a while when he spoke, the person closest to him was sprayed with saliva. My grandmother was short and skinny with a heavily wrinkled face—and her hair was pulled back in a severe bun. Rosemary was the only one who looked like she belonged to this century. She was about thirty-three but she looked more like forty-five, heavily wrinkled like her mother. Both my grandmother and Rosemary held cigarettes in their hands and puffed greedily.

When Mama introduced me to Paw Paw he looked me up and down with a disgusted expression and said, "Out here only cheap women do their hair like that. We'll have to get you some dye so you don't look like a floozy!"

Huh? Lots of Hollywood female celebrities bleached their hair! Hadn't he heard of Doris Day, Marilyn Monroe and so many others?

I looked at Mama waiting for her to come to my defense but she looked away and said nothing.

Then he turned to my brothers seeing their shaggy heads and said "I'm gonna take my clippers to you!"

Frankie looked at him with a defiant gleam in his eyes and I knew immediately this was not going to be the vacation I'd dreamed of. Oh well. It was only two weeks. Maybe we could stay out of Paw Paw's way.

Rosemary guided us to her car, a 1959 Ford, and then drove us to Paw Paw's house—a cheap, small, dilapidated, two bedroom shack in Pinedale, which was a very low income suburb of Fresno. I found out later, Pinedale was originally Camp Pinedale during World War II. Now it was one of the scummiest places in the area to live.

The house itself was dirty and smelled of grease and unwashed bodies. My mother's two youngest sisters and brother were teenagers, just a little older than me and the five of them lived crammed together here. I wondered where we were going to sleep while we visited. I also wondered how they were able to send us the money for our vacation if they lived like this.

During the next few days, my brothers and I were pretty much ignored by the adults. Mama slept on the couch and we slept on pallets on the floor in the tiny front room. I got along okay with the teenagers but they had been raised in an old-fashioned fundamentalist religion that said the girls couldn't cut their hair, wear makeup, etc. Plus, they'd never worked anywhere but the fields, cutting grapes, picking cotton, and neither had ever been on a date, so we had very little in common. There was absolutely nothing to do. Paw Paw didn't have a car. He walked back and forth every day to his janitor's job at a manufacturing plant in Pinedale. They got to the grocery store and church via Rosemary or their other daughter, Margie—the one who'd lived with us for a while in Greenville before Mama married Menard. Margie had moved back to California the year before with her new husband Bill.

I asked Mama how we were going to go to Hollywood and Yosemite.

She shrugged.

"We'll figure out something later."

By the end of the third day, I was ready to go home. The filth, and odor in the one bathroom, the dirty clothes that everyone walked on in the bedrooms, the insults from Paw Paw—he'd harped on my hair and my smoking, told my brother Frankie at least five times that he'd end up in prison by the time he was twenty-one—and the covert staring that all of the adults seemed to do, was getting on my nerves. Plus, I was used to working. Here, I was cooped up with all of them twenty-four hours a day. And they didn't like us kids any better than we liked them! So that made TWO sets of grandparents who treated us terribly!

By the seventh day I began asking Mama when we were leaving. It couldn't be too soon for me.

"Pretty soon," she answered. "Pretty soon."

Everybody except Paw Paw remained silent.

"What did you lose in Texas?" he sneered. "What is it that you need to get back there to?"

"My job and my friends," I answered.

On the tenth day I began to get worried. Mama wasn't doing anything to get ready to go and nobody was saying any goodbyes. I couldn't help but think about my job. Junior would hire someone else if I wasn't back on time and I not only needed that job; I liked it. My friends made sure I got home at night. If I lost that job, how was I going to get back and forth to work? I didn't want to go back to Rockyfellers.

"When are we going home?" I asked Mama again.

"Oh, I can't remember. I'll have to look it up," she said

"Well . . . look it up! I want to know," I insisted.

Paw Paw and Mama Davis stared at the T. V. screen where their favorite soap opera, General Hospital flickered. But it was obvious they were more interested in what was being said between me and Mama. My three aunts and uncle were at school.

"Oh, I don't want to get up right now. I'll do it later," Mama said again.

By now I was beside myself. I'd taken all the flak I could take from these people and I was going stir crazy. I wanted to know when we were getting the heck out and back to some sort of normalcy.

"I want to know now," I insisted. I stood my ground with hands on hips.

Paw Paw turned his head and glared at me.

"You're too big for your britches, little girl. Somebody ought to whip your tail a time or two and you just might become a pretty good kid!" he threatened.

He started to stand.

I ignored him.

"I want to know when we're getting out of here. They don't want us here. We should never have come!" I yelled at my mother.

Paw Paw stood up menacingly.

Mama finally looked at him and said weakly, "Daddy, I'll handle it."

He sat back down.

"She needs a little taste of my strap," he said.

"Mama avoided my eyes but murmured, "We're not going back."

I was sure I'd misunderstood.

"What?" I demanded.

"We're not going back to Dallas. We're staying here."

I heard a faint ringing in my ears and felt dizzy. I looked around the room at Paw Paw who was sitting back in his recliner with a triumphant smirk on his face. Mama Davis was looking at the floor, her shoulders and head down. Frankie and Gary were staring at Mama with panic on their faces.

Frankie blurted out, "We're staying here with THEM?"

He nodded his head toward our grandparents, his eyes pleading for Mama to say no, it was all a mistake.

Gary looked stricken.

My first thought was, as bad as it had been, Dallas had been a picnic compared to the way we had been treated here. As young as they were, the two boys knew it too.

"When did you decide that? And why didn't you ask how we felt about it?" I was crying now. "I don't want to stay here! What about my job?"

Mama wouldn't respond. She was intent on the same program Paw Paw had been watching.

"You never intended to go back home did you?" I accused, and could see from her face that I'd hit on the truth. "It was all a lie from the beginning!"

"Why?!" I wailed.

She remained silent.

I said it again.

"WHY?!"

"Because I knew you'd throw a fit," she admitted.

"Throw a fit?" I sobbed. "You didn't even let us tell Daddy or any of our friends goodbye!"

"Your daddy don't give a Fig Newton about y'all!" Paw Paw growled.

I whirled on him.

"Oh! And you do?!" I screamed, facing him down.

By this time Mama had rushed over and had her arms around me in a restraining manner. Frankie and Gary were crying. The babies watched us anxiously.

"I sent you the money to come out here, didn't I?" he countered. Now he was standing with his meaty finger pointed in my face, spewing saliva everywhere.

"You didn't send ME anything! The two of you had this all worked out with no input whatsoever from me!"

I was hysterical.

I broke away from Mama and ran out the front door. I didn't know where I was going. I headed down Minarets Street. I hadn't been anywhere in this God-forsaken place, so I just ran. I heard Paw Paw yelling.

"You get back here this minute young lady!"

And then Mama's voice: "Let her alone, Daddy. Where's she gonna go?"

I kept running.

Yeah, where was I going to go?

I had no money and no way to get any. I'd already discovered that in California you had to be sixteen years old and enrolled in school before you could get a work permit, even for part time work. I'd quit school in the beginning of the ninth grade so if I returned in September I'd be three years behind others in my age group. I didn't think I could stand the humiliation.

I stumbled on until I couldn't run anymore, then sat down on the curb and sobbed. I could write to Daddy and he'd send the money for me to get home just to spite Mama but I didn't want to live with him either. He was now living in Pickton, ninety-three miles from my friends and my job in Dallas. Besides, even if he sent money, they'd take it away from me. I was stuck. And so angry!

Mama had devised a deliberate lie. Why? Why couldn't she have told me? I was old enough to be working full-time to help with the financial obligations of the family, but not old enough to be told the truth about such a life-changing move? I knew I couldn't have stayed behind. There was no way I could have completely supported myself. But at least I could have said my goodbyes, gotten addresses and phone numbers to keep in touch with my friends.

I thought of James. I had planned to see him again, as soon as I screwed my courage up. Now, I'd never get to tell him how I felt. And he would think I just dumped him.

Then there was Doyle, who had been so funny and made the last several weeks of my life in Dallas such fun. He'd shown me that laughing was good for the soul. I'd just started to get to know him but now that was over.

Well, at least I wouldn't have to go back home and admit to my friends that I hadn't gotten anywhere near Hollywood. I'd been worrying about how I'd face people after bragging about all the stars I'd see.

And then I remembered my Hi Fi, records, radio, and stuffed blue dog. With no money, how was I going to get them out here? I didn't turn sixteen until September. That was a little over five months away. Would a school give me a work permit then, even if I wasn't in school? I didn't know. What was I going to do between now and then? I hated the thought of living with these people that long.

After a while I stood and slowly started walking back the way I'd come. When I got back to the house I walked straight to Mama and asked her about my stuff.

"When we get some money the Preacher will send your things," she said.

"How long is that going to be?" I asked.

"I'm going to start looking for a job soon."

"And what are we," I nodded at my siblings, "supposed to do while you're working?"

"Behave and try to make yourselves useful," she said, still avoiding my eyes.

I looked around at the crowded, filthy house. She'd better not mean we were supposed to do something about that. That house hadn't been cleaned in years.

"You'll see. It'll be okay. You'll get used to it," she said.

"Is that supposed to make what you did all right?" I shot back.

"We were starving to death in Dallas," she said. "We couldn't keep living that way."

I didn't have an answer for that. But I didn't see how things were going to be any different here. Except now, we were living with people who didn't like us and didn't mind if we knew it. And I didn't even have my music.

It was years after our arrival in California before we were able to afford anything but basic necessities. I was twenty years old before I got to drive through Hollywood. It was a huge disappointment. I was twenty-two when I got to visit Yosemite. And Mama had nothing to do with me being able to go anywhere!

Chapter Eleven

The day after I turned sixteen in September, I lied about my age again and applied for a job at a Dairy Delight that offered only window service. They didn't ask for an I. D. My second payday I cashed my check and got the Preacher's phone number from Mama. I was going to find out how much money I needed to send him so that he would put my stuff in the mail.

After three rings the operator came on and informed me the phone had been disconnected with no forwarding number. There were no other people with his first and last name or first initial listed and nothing under Preachers or Ministers. We never heard from him again. Needless to say I never got back my treasures. I had to wonder if Mama had given him my stuff to help pay back the grocery money she'd borrowed. I wondered if she'd even given me his real name. I asked those questions but knew I couldn't trust anything she said.

In California I struggled for the next many years just to survive. It seemed my life was over before it had even started. Depression overwhelmed me. I muddled along with no joy, no light at the end of the tunnel, and no hope for the future.

I was thankful for my Dairy Delight job but couldn't see working in a drive inn for the rest of my life. I was sixteen years old and had no one but myself to count on. I had no education, no skills, no confidence, no hope, and no path to escape my miserable existence.

But, I didn't have to worry about working a long time at the Dairy Delight. Four months after I got that job Mama moved us clear across town and I had to quit. I worked at night and had no way to get home at midnight. Our next house was on a major street in between two businesses. I was once again stuck in a horrible house/neighborhood with no way to get anywhere. I had a lot of time to think.

It wasn't just a better job. I wanted to like myself and didn't! I longed to become a better person; honest and upstanding like some of my heroes I watched on the big screen and two or three people like my old friends Harry Lee and Mary Drinning that I'd had the privilege of knowing early in my life.

I hated cheaters and liars—probably because I'd been lied to all my life. I wanted to earn people's respect. I wanted to develop and maintain high principles and stand by them no matter what. Yet I wasn't any of those things—I found myself falling back into the same easy-outs that my parents and grandparents had used whenever they got into difficult situations. A lot of my lies and short comings were because I didn't want to hurt anyone's feelings or make them feel badly. I'd always been for the "underdog" even way back at Linfield School when I'd tried to help the mean girls' side-kick. But some I'm ashamed to admit—way too many—were because I didn't have the guts to own up and take responsibility!

I was even fired from a job because I didn't want to hurt the owners' son's feelings! I was seventeen, the son was eighteen. I was the morning shift waitress at the restaurant. He was a morning grill cook. He was also a pasty-looking nerd, with lackluster personality, barely communicated except to announce "order up". He apparently developed a crush on me and got up enough courage to ask me out. I was shocked, I'd had no clue. I felt uncomfortable working with him! I certainly didn't want to go on a date! BUT I didn't want to make him feel bad! (I'd do this several more times in the future with guys I had no interest in mainly because I felt sorry for them.) So I said yes. He said he'd pick me up the next evening at a certain time.

I was miserable. I did NOT want to go out with him. Couldn't imagine even giving him a quick peck of a kiss at the end of the evening! So, spineless me waited till the last minute and pleaded "sick". I didn't go. And, by that cowardly act I hurt him anyway! I didn't like myself but honestly I was relieved. I didn't have to pretend for several hours to be interested in him.

Well, I SHOULD have called in sick to work the next morning, but didn't. I went in at my usual time, six a.m. The pasty-looking guy didn't show up. Right after the lunch hour rush the bosses, the nerd's father AND mother, called me into the office and fired me. Of course, they gave some made up excuse—I'd never had any complaints or warnings before that day—but they and I both knew they were upset I'd stood up their son!

I already knew, as a teenager, it didn't matter what your reasons or excuses were. EVERYBODY had "reasons" for the rotten or cowardly things they did. Mama's "reason" for lying about the California "vacation" (and so many other things) was because it was *much easier* for her to pull it off with no resistance. I recognized I was taking the same path my mother (and other family members) had followed—and hated myself for it—but hadn't yet learned how to change my course, even though I didn't want to be like them!

I told myself if I could get into a better job I might feel better about myself—maybe a higher class restaurant where I could waitress. I found one, and then another and another for the next several years but hated them as well. Then I thought what I needed was a good job as a sales clerk in a department store. For some reason I thought that job showed a little more "class" than being a waitress. I went to work at Woolworth's and then Longs Drugstore but that didn't do it for me either. I was living on my own by that time though and did feel much better about that. I'd separated myself from my abusive grandparents and shirt tail relatives at age seventeen. But I still would go see, and call Mama a couple times a month. I kept hoping!

Then someone rear-ended me in my old '62 Chevy II that I'd saved and bought toward the end of my sixteenth year.

When I called home from the wreck site to tell my mother I'd been in a wreck her first response was, "Oh My God, is the car okay?" I'd like to say I was used to responses like that but it was just another chip off my heart—she didn't ask if I was okay. It was years later that I brought that up and she did then what she'd always done; denied she'd ever said anything like that.

My insurance company awarded fourteen hundred dollars, more than my car was actually worth, for a whiplash and damages. The Judge on the case put the money in a trust with my mother as guardian, and suggested I use it for some sort of schooling. I mulled that idea over for a while and decided I'd use if for beauty school—I didn't need a high school diploma for that. Mama signed half the money over to Lyle's Beauty College to cover the first few months. The Judge had decreed that I had to finish half the beauty course and then I'd get the rest for the remaining tuition.

I got started. Mama had promised she'd drive me to and from school. OR, let me use her car when she didn't need it. I moved back in with her and the kids. They lived in Pinedale in a house next door to her parents. Beauty school was in downtown Fresno which was eleven miles from where we lived.

That transportation commitment from Mama lasted two and a half months. It was winter and one day when the rain was lashing down and wind blowing I waited outside the entrance for her to pick me up. The school was closed, everybody else gone long ago. I waited an hour. We still didn't have a phone. I had no money so I had no choice but to start walking.

I cried out of rage the entire time but managed to cover about six miles to a friend's apartment. I stopped to ask them if I could rest there a while. They said of course. I tried calling my grandparents to locate Mama. They'd seen her but she'd taken off somewhere without saying where she was going. OH I HATED HER SO MUCH!!

I spent the night on my friends' couch. I called my grandparents again the next morning and Mama just happened to be there. They put her on the phone. I was still so angry and hurt.

"Where were you yesterday?" I asked in an elevated voice I'm sure.

"I forgot," she answered.

"What could have come up that you couldn't remember you were supposed to pick me up? This has been a daily occurrence, six days a week for almost three months!"

She had no answer. I could imagine her responding as she usually did when she got caught in a lie or failing to live up to her responsibilities; that pursing of her lips, clenching of her jaw, and silence.

I admit I let her have a piece of my mind (no cursing or anything like that—I didn't use bad language! But I sure didn't "bless" her either.) She hung up on me without bothering to ask if I was okay or even where I was. Oh well, nothing new but it still hurt.

I stayed at my friends' for the next three days. I decided to quit beauty school. That wasn't ALL Mama's fault. I already knew I wasn't beautician material, not because I couldn't do it. I could. As a matter of fact I was pretty good at it. I just didn't like it! I couldn't see spending any more money, muddling through something I knew wasn't for me, ESPECIALLY since I had no guaranteed way to get back and forth! But what WAS for me? I had no clue. There were several "empty holes" in me and I didn't know how to fill up any of them.

Then I decided I'd get a job as an office clerk. For unknown reasons I thought that was more respectable or something. But I had no education so didn't know how to go about it.

I found a fee-for-referral employment agency who found an entry-level clerical job in a major insurance company for me. I had to pay the employment agency three hundred dollars out of my first few checks—which was almost my whole month's salary. What a rip off! It took only a couple of months to know I wouldn't be able to do that work very long. I couldn't stand being caged inside an office tied to a desk doing the same old paper work over and over again, day after day, week after week. I had no hope of promotions because of my lack of an education.

What was wrong with me?! Why couldn't I find some kind of work I could do and feel some sort of satisfaction? Why couldn't I be happy? What was it going to take to cause me to lose the depression and "born to lose" attitude? Maybe I wasn't meant to be happy? Was that just my lot in life? It sure seemed so. I went back to waitressing because I'd discovered I liked that more than the other jobs I'd tried, although I couldn't fathom how I'd be able to do it my entire life. I didn't know at that time that a different "job" would not change my life or do what I needed to happen. I'd learn after a while that if you want a better life you have to BE better, AND DO better!

Turns out it was PARTLY my mother, without even trying to, or knowing that she did, who blazed the trail to a better life for me. She'd been on Welfare beginning two years after we arrived in California when she got pregnant with her sixth child and got dumped immediately by the father. At that time the requirements for welfare assistance was that an able bodied parent had to attend school or training of some sort. She was forced into school a half a day, three days a week, at a daytime adult school created specifically for welfare recipients. She eventually got her high school diploma. From there she finished two years at the local community college.

In the meantime, while she was at the junior college, I started adult school four nights a week to earn my high school diploma while working as a waitress during the day. A big part of the reason I gave it a chance was because Mama was showing me it could be done by people from our station in life.

But another huge influence was a middle-aged educator I liked and respected, who shocked me into reality by responding to my excuse: "It would take me nine or ten years to get through high school and college—I'd be twenty-nine years old when I graduated!"

He had looked at me silently for a moment and then said, "Well, how old will you be in nine or ten years if you DON'T go through high school and college?!"

That woke me up! I got serious. When I was handed my high school diploma I was also informed that I had earned a small scholarship to the local community college.

As I continued school I watched Mama's progress. She transferred from the community college and enrolled at Cal State University, Fresno. She earned her B. A. degree and then spent another year earning her teaching credential. I couldn't believe her choice of study! She had ignored, neglected and even abused and allowed abuse of her own children but her "heart's desire" was to work with little children?! She still had three sub teens of her own at home that she continued to ignore! My hope was that she had recognized her mistakes with all of us, had turned over a new leaf, and was going to make amends for the past.

No such luck. She did land a very good teaching job almost immediately at a coastal men's prison, making more money than either of us would have ever imagined. She parted ways with the bum she'd been shacking with in Fresno (this was the longest relationship she'd ever had besides my father) and moved to that new area. She settled herself and the three youngest kids into a very nice townhouse. I was so proud and hopeful that things were turning around for her and the kids.

In the meantime, I finished community college earning another small scholarship and transferred to Cal State Fresno. To be able to attend the four year college I scrimped and saved, took out school loans (that took me fifteen years to pay off) got financial assistance from various programs, and even a one-time two hundred dollar "loan" from my father (believe it or not!)

I was learning that the only sure way to build a positive self-image and self-confidence was to stick my neck out, take risks, stand up for my beliefs and rights; to "reach for the stars", and rejoice over my victories and accomplishments. I was beginning to see the light at the end of the tunnel. I was beginning to respect myself!

But Mama committed an act that caused me to lose even more respect! Before her six month probationary period at the prison was up she got involved with an inmate named Dino who was only two years older than me! She and the other trainees had been warned against this in orientation many times because it was so common. But she did what she always did—"damn the rules". She fell for it, hook line and sinker!

The Con was being released on parole and convinced her that he was in love with her so she invited him to move in (with three preteen children in the home; two girls and one boy!). She gave him her credit cards, the keys to her new Datsun Honeybee that she'd only had a couple of months, and turned him loose while she worked. It took the prison only a couple of weeks to find out about her new "live-in love". She was fired immediately and her California teaching credential was ripped to shreds. She would never be able to teach in a public school again.

Suffice it to say I was shocked, extremely disappointed, and embarrassed. Thank God, no one in my circle of friends had ever met my mother or any of my family! At that point we lived in different cities almost three hours apart.

Yet, I wondered if I was crazy—*WHY do I keep hoping that she will change and become the mother that I and my siblings long for?*

I was in my middle twenties at that time but still ached for a loving parent. I was depressed over that for a long time. Not just for me but for my brothers and sisters, the youngest three who needed her the most. She'd spent YEARS in school to obtain her high school diploma, then an A. A. and B. A. degree with cum laude honors, and a California Teaching Credential—neglecting her youngest kids to focus on studies while she did it. It was gone in a blink of an eye!

She'd also made a couple of good teacher friends who were in orientation with her. That in itself was impressive—she'd never before had any real friends that lasted over a couple of weeks! I'd been so excited and happy for her. But in less than six months of graduation she flushed everything down the toilet—including the friends—for a prison inmate twenty-something years her junior after having been WARNED they'd try to con the teachers (any employee) into establishing a relationship, and if that happened, the teacher would be immediately terminated, possibly even prosecuted.

It was exactly four weeks later that the Con dumped Mama and moved on. But first he'd talked Mama into buying and installing a new C B radio in her little car for him. She'd given him her credit cards which he promptly maxed out and put an enormous amount of miles on her car. She went into her depressed, but hostile "I didn't do anything wrong, it's the State of California—they don't care about helping people! They are the culprits here!" mode.

In her "book" (which I will explain in the next chapter) on page 26 she says: *"My teaching career ended because of ill health."* If it wasn't so sick and sad, it MIGHT be funny! But there are too many legal records on file detailing what really happened! Just ANOTHER bald-faced lie!

She did manage to find a job fairly soon after being fired by the prison. She went to work in that same city a tad above minimum wage as a cook in a senior citizens center. Of course she had to move back into a shack with the kids. She worked that job for about six years, long enough to meet two different bums—and when I say "bums" I mean one of them was a real alcoholic street bum she'd met in the hospital when she went to pray for the sick. She thought she could turn him around and get him on the straight and narrow. She married him within a couple of months! That marriage lasted a matter of weeks. He quickly decided he liked the street life better than her!

The second was a grossly obese senior citizen, nicknamed Tiny, who frequented the Center for lunches. She moved Tiny into her home. That didn't last long either.

Approximately eight years later she did get a job in a very small private school teaching third graders (you only needed a B. A. degree, not a credential, in order to teach there) but that only lasted a few months. The Administrator stated she started acting hostile to suggestions and requirements of the job. From there she went to part time clerical and sales clerk jobs until she was able to retire on Social Security.

I continued in my quest for a better life. At first I didn't think I'd make it—didn't think I was smart enough. But I LOVED school, loved learning—any and everything, EXCEPT math! But, I even made it through that with flying colors.

In 1976 I graduated magna cum laude with my B.A. Degree. I Immediately went to work in the criminal justice field for a couple of years and then worked under the control and direction of licensed investigators as a paid apprentice for the next two years which qualified me to take the California state test as a Private Investigator. I passed with flying colors.

I thought I'd found my purpose in life! I was not just making up Nancy Drew type mysteries as I had in fifth grade; I was actually investigating REAL mysteries! I loved the work and was very good at it. Never—well almost never—a boring day. And the money wasn't bad either. But I wanted more, and knew I had more in me—exactly what, I wasn't sure.

I returned to the university and earned my California Adult Teaching Credential and taught in three different adult school districts, all kinds of classes, for ten years. I loved that too!

But in my early forties I found what I was MEANT to do—my absolute purpose in life! I started writing again. I started with humorous stories from my childhood—which were few and far between but very important to me. Then I went on just to write my memories, good and bad. I was proud of the results. One day I showed Mama the funny ones and she laughed and laughed through each one. I told her I was thinking about trying to get them published.

She handed back my notebook and said with a very somber face and serious voice, "Yeah, they're funny to us, but they wouldn't mean anything to anybody else. Nobody wants to read about a plain ordinary person. They only want to read stories about celebrities like Carol Burnett." (The book of Carol Burnett's life story had just been released and was all the rage).

I am so thankful I FINALLY didn't listen to her!! I was not going to allow her to interfere in my dream and my future! I kept writing and before too many weeks had passed I submitted a story to The Fresno Bee. They loved it and published it the very next Sunday on the front page of the community section. I got phone calls from strangers off and on all day that day, telling me how inspiring they thought my story was. (I was in the phone book and still using my unusual married name.) I couldn't believe the response!

Two days later I got a call from a local published author who taught writing for publication classes in our area. She told me how wonderful my article was.

Her exact words were, "You've got talent, Lady!"

She then invited me to an upcoming writers' convention—I didn't even know there were such things! And further, she invited me to join her classes. I attended the convention where I knew absolutely NO ONE but from the moment it commenced I was in absolute HEAVEN! I KNEW I was supposed to be there!

I signed up for the Author's classes that day and began to learn, over the next year and a half, the difference between writing papers in high school and college and writing for publication. There is a HUGE difference! I went on to publish in numerous magazines, newspapers, journals, etc.

Finally, in 2003, through trial and error, I put together that book I'd known was in me since early grade school. The title was *Time & Again* and it was a novel based on a true story. However the first section designated as "Dallas, Texas" (approximately 80 pages) was my true story, even though I'd changed all the names and identifying information.

When *Time & Again* was released my mother, my siblings, and I had been estranged for more than fifteen years. (I'd severed relationships with the grandparents and most of the aunts and uncles in the mid-sixties.) I'd have maybe two or three brief phone calls every couple of months with my mother. I'd even moved to Tennessee for a year and then moved back to California. I'd never introduced my mother to my California friends and none of them knew anything about my history.

My family knew absolutely nothing about me but they sure made up a lot of stuff! For instance, I was told one of my brothers who I hadn't seen or had a conversation with since 1988 had told my father that I was making so much money as an investigator that I was getting brand new cars every year and if one of them broke down on the highway, my company would just leave the car there on the side of the road and immediately send me out another brand new one! The only tiny bit of truth in that was my company was providing a brand new car every TWO years but I covered a four thousand square mile territory of Central California by myself and was on the road all day every day of the week. I put a lot of miles on my cars. Some of the other "Linda stories" were even more outrageous than that!

Well, my mother heard about my book through a relative, got a copy, recognized herself, and threw a fit—at first behind my back.

Her first personal message to me was a "syrupy-sweet": "Well, I hope you make a million dollars, the book has everything, love, heartbreak, pathos . . . I'm sure it will be a bestseller and you've worked very hard all your life for this."

Behind my back to everybody else who'd listen: my siblings, nieces, nephews, friends of relatives, etc., she was saying in a loud angry tone: "Well, I hope Linda makes a million dollars on her book because money's all she's ever cared about anyway!"

Of course word got back to me from several people. Some who just wanted to gossip and cause trouble. Some like my youngest sister and one niece who wanted to, and did tell me, how horrible and what a liar I was. The niece added that I was just "jealous of" my mother. All because of the stuff my mother was telling them.

Finally, Mama had the guts to call me and say: "Well, you sure didn't make me look good!"

I thought: *NO! YOU didn't make YOU look good when you did all those things!*

Instead I told her, "It's a NOVEL. It says that prominently on the front cover. All the names are changed. I'm not telling people it has anything to do with me. If you don't say anything no one will ever connect it to you!"

But she couldn't let it go. She could NEVER allow anyone to think she did anything wrong! She always had to be the "perfect" one and everybody else was the liar and villain.

She went on the war path.

She told my siblings, nieces and nephews that I was "making up lies" and trying to make her look bad. I just blocked their emails and phone calls and let it go. They all had serious problems: mental, emotional, drugs, alcohol, etc. They KNEW some of the things she'd done like ignoring and neglecting them all their lives, moving the ex con in and getting fired from the prison, moving the two bums in later on, lying to them all the time, etc., but chose to erase all that stuff from their memories. They decided to go for my throat!

Chapter Twelve

One year later, in 2004, Mama was still stewing in fury and lusting for revenge. She decided to write her own "book" to tell what a hard life she'd had and how hard she'd worked to become the great person that she was. She said she was doing it for "Ministry purposes". She wanted to help people who were going through horrible things—to let them know they could overcome anything—just like she did. She was going to get it published and then turn it over to a Ministry.

But she warned everyone NOT to let three people know anything about her book: Me (and my children), Margie, and Rebecca—two of her sisters who knew her history and how she operated).

Why the secrecy? Because Margie would know about Mama's childhood years. Both Margie and I would KNOW all about the Texas circumstances. All three of us would have first-hand knowledge of the things that occurred in California after 1963 when Mama moved us there.

I found out about Mama's "book" after all the copies had been distributed to my siblings and other maternal relatives. My information came from Margie who'd lived with us in Greenville, had met Bud Abbott, and introduced Mama to Menard. I'm not positive but I think it was Mama's younger sister, Rebecca that obtained a copy of the book Mama gave to my sister Karen. Rebecca had read it and called Margie (who had already read *Time & Again*, loved it, and agreed it was right on true (at least the parts that Margie had been a personal witness to). Now Margie was determined to read Mama's "book", ESPECIALLY because Mama had ordered that she was not to be told about it!

For once I was glad that family loved to spread gossip.

Margie received a copy and promptly forwarded one to me. She also compiled a long, many-paged critique of Mama's "book" pointing out all the things that were NOT TRUE, of which she (Margie) had first-hand knowledge.

Margie was there for much of Mama's childhood. Margie introduced her to Menard and witnessed their wedding. Margie was there when they moved us to Dallas AND, she had knowledge that Mama was hijacking us to California long before it happened. From that point on until the mid-1980's Margie was there! She knew my mother well.

Of course, my younger siblings, nieces, nephews, brothers and sisters-in law were too young to know or remember, hadn't been around, or hadn't even been born when a lot of the rotten stuff happened.

Karen and Terry were just babies when they'd been farmed out to a stranger (Dora, the babysitter) for a year and a half so, of course, they couldn't remember it. Frankie and Gary didn't remember the details of Mama lying and "kidnapping" us to California—Frankie had been ten and Gary only eight. Margie stepped in to make sure the truth was out.

This time, Mama was NOT going to get away with a revision of her history! Margie even went so far as to have her typed critique notarized and sent me a copy.

When I received my copy of Mama's "book" (66 typed pages) I read and marked paragraph after paragraph on every page that I knew to be a flat out lie, exaggeration, or things that had happened to someone else that Mama was now pretending had happened to her!

Her entire "book" was laid out to make her look like the long suffering victim who overcame impossible odds and practically saved the world! Most of the incidents in the "book" were things that only family members—my mother's older siblings, her mother and father, my father, Margie (who was "on the scene" from childhood to sometime in the mid-eighties), Menard, me and my two brothers, etc., would know about. But many of those people, including my brother Frankie, were dead.

The title of her book was "Surrounded by Angels" and it starts, ends and is heavily interspersed with scriptures and thanks to God for his protection of her, etc., etc. She changed everybody's names except my father's. I was "Laura". She goes on and on about how she "poured out all her pent up love" on me, and did everything she could to make my life easier!

She describes herself throughout as *"a strong, faith-filled, Christian woman, who struggled to survive and raise my kids by the Grace of God"*. She dictated the story to one of her grandsons' girlfriends (who was a foreign student that had just recently met Mama and knew nothing about her). The student typed it up and then took it to Kinko's Copy Center, had copies made, had them spiral bound for all Mama's OTHER children, their wives, husbands, and grandkids. Mama hand wrote a "dedication" or the person's name on the front "cover".

Mama's first paragraph reads: *"My intent in writing this narrative is not to cast aspersions on anyone, but to state as accurately and plainly as possible, the incidents and highlights of my life that helped to form my personality and to instill in me the deep conviction that I am never alone, and that no matter how terrible the situation in life may seem there is reason to rejoice and praise The Lord."*

Then she goes on to take many things that happened to other people, especially her siblings—and a lot that happened to me (she must have poured through my book one page at a time!) and claimed those incidents happened to her.

For instance:

Page 1: she claims Her Aunt Vera (Beth in her book—the one we visited for holiday dinners in Sulphur Springs—told her that when she (Mama) was two weeks old, Paw Paw spanked her so hard for crying that she was bruised on her lower body for weeks.

Now, that could be true—her parents were CRAZY and abusive! And, if Paw Paw would do it once he could do it again.

But Margie says it was Rebecca at three months old who Paw Paw spanked at church and was subsequently caught and chastised by the Preacher and others. Margie was an eye witness the day of baby Rebecca's whipping. NOBODY ever said a word that he had ever done that before to another child in the family.

Page 3: says *"At seven years old . . . little girls wore short pretty dresses, short curly hair and bobby socks . . . I was forced to wear long, plain dresses that reached below my knees, long sleeves, long cotton stockings and long plaited hair. The other kids all laughed at me and no one wanted to play with me."*

Mama would have been seven in 1934 which was the middle of the Great Depression and they were living in a poor, sparsely-populated farming area of Texas. A check of history records will show that in 1934 the majority of little girls in extremely rural areas like that were NOT wearing short dresses, short curly hair, and ABSOLUTELY WERE NOT wearing "bobby socks"!!

Bobby socks came into production and popularity in the mid 1940's. They became very popular in the 1950's which was my era. I mentioned them a couple of times in my book! She mentions "bobby socks" again on page 7, paragraph 3.

Page 8: Mama claims she came down with Malaria and suffered terribly from that disease for several years. Margie says it was her (Margie) that contracted Malaria. Margie never heard a peep of Mama or any of her other siblings having it.

Page 9: she claims she incurred a deep cut on her leg by a sharpened hoe, and another cut to the bone of her leg by an axe for which her parents wouldn't take her to a doctor. Margie says both of those accidents happened to her. Margie was the one with the scars to prove it—the axe-cut to the bone left a two inch scar Margie has to this day.

Of course the above four family stories could have happened before Margie was born; she was eleven years younger than Mama, but you'd think someone might have said when Margie came down with Malaria, and got a hoe cut and an axe cut to her legs, "Oh, well I'll be! Fay had that, or did that, too!" Nobody ever did.

But the following cannot be argued away:

Page 6, paragraph 2: Mama talks about her mother being cold and aloof and jealous of her (Mama's) love for her father.

Mama accused me at age thirteen of trying to sleep with her new boyfriend Gene because he felt badly for me and bought me a coat!

Then on page 16, paragraph 2 Mama goes on about my coat situation: *". . . a group of Christmas Carolers came by our apartment and gave me* (Mama) *a check for $70."*

First, we lived in low-income rooming/boarding houses—we NEVER had Christmas Carolers serenade us!

Second, how many groups of Christmas Carolers have you ever heard of that hand out checks? Or even cash for that matter! Were the checks blank and the Carolers filled in the name of the recipient when they decided on one? Or was Mama's name already on the check and if so, how did they get her name? None of this is believable!

But this is the "kicker": *"That evening a group of Carolers . . . came by our apartment and gave us a tree and a check for seventy dollars. Laura,* (Me!) *who had gone all winter without a coat, begged me for the money so she could buy a coat. I gave her the entire check. She* (Me!) *told me later, 'Mama, I thought this was going to be a miserable Christmas, but it has actually been very nice.' We had Rocky burgers* (she got this from my book!) *instead of turkey, but it was a pretty good holiday that year."*

BEGGED? I NEVER begged my mother OR my father for ANYTHING! I learned at a very young age that could cause me terrible pain—either emotional, physical or BOTH! I never asked her for anything—I tried to take care of my needs myself! The closest I ever came to "begging" was when she made me go to a phone booth and call my father to ask for a "loan" for food when we all had the flu! And it did no good. Besides, why would a responsible mother whose children are starving to death give a seventy dollar check to a teenager whose "begging" for the money, when they ALL need food?! Makes no sense at all!

The truth was she lost her boyfriend Gene over nasty accusations she made about him and me just because he took pity on me and bought me a coat that winter!

Also, we NEVER had a Christmas tree or decorations in Dallas or in California either, as long as I lived at home! We never even had presents unless someone outside of our family gave them to us! As far as dinner that Christmas Day—she wasn't even home with us! I remember it well!

Then on page 16: she fabricates a story about my blue, stuffed dog that Pete Hensley gave me for Christmas! She says: *". . . I walked three miles through the snow from work to our apartment, on one particular day. Shortly after I arrived home I received a phone call from one of the girls at work. She said that the Salvation Army was distributing toys to needy children for the next five days. I called my supervisor and told him that I would be absent the next day because I was going to attend the Salvation Army's Toy distribution center. When I was ushered into the storage room I found a three foot stuffed dog that I chose for Laura (Me!) . . ."*

First of all, we NEVER HAD A PHONE! Nobody could have called her from work to notify her of ANYTHING! We didn't even have a phone in California for at least five or more years after we arrived! The day she "forgot" to pick me up at Beauty School I was almost eighteen years old and we still didn't have a phone!

That blue stuffed dog was the ONLY stuffed animal I ever got and my boyfriend Pete gave it to me for Christmas in 1961! Why a giant, blue stuffed dog? I don't know but I treasured it even after Pete and I broke up. Mama, of course, caused me to lose it when she made me leave it with some man while she "took us on a vacation to California"!

On page 17, paragraph 3: she tells a story about how some customer from work (Rockyfeller's, Walnut Hill) offered to take her home and instead drove her out to a swampy, garbage dump area and *"told me his intentions"*. She says he told her *"It won't do you any good to scream because there is no one within miles to hear you."*

That idea came straight from my book where I related the incident of the college guy, Tommy, who pulled that trick—with different words—on me! I had several relatives who knew her and had read both *Time & Again* as well as Mama's "book" tell me they thought she was so jealous of me that she tried to be me!

Page 14: she says this regarding during and after her divorce from my father: *"The year that followed was a bleak one. I had no social life. Dad* (Paw Paw) *had moved the family to Fresno, California* (they moved to California in 1950—her divorce was when I was ten—1957!) *to be near my brother, Frank* (Elmer). *I went to work in a small café. We didn't live high on the hog, but we got by on a slim budget. I met and married my second husband, Lynn,* (Menard) *the following year . . ."*

Once again, no cigar! She flipped over Bud Abbot BEFORE her divorce was even started! When he dumped her she ran straight for a guy (Menard) who didn't even know enough to brush his teeth and take regular baths!

She goes on to say she had two children by Menard and divorced him when she *". . . found out he was having an affair with a co-worker"*.

But remember I was there! Mama dumped Menard! He did NOT have an affair! Truthfully, I don't think he was smart enough to get involved in affair. I think SHE was having an affair, or at least trying to! She was hanging around with an old scuzzy, nasty-mouthed woman and man at that time and they were going out a lot! Mama treated Menard worse than a human should be treated, and that's coming from someone (Me) who didn't like Menard at all!

Then she says, she ". . . *gave birth to a daughter, Julia,* (April) *who "was born after our* (hers and Menard's) *divorce".*

Nope! She TRIES to make it sound as if "Julia" was Menard's baby.

A HUGE LIE!! "Julia" (April) was born approximately two years <u>after</u> we arrived in California as a result of Mama's short tryst with a married truck driver she'd met where she worked. The baby was a beautiful, sweet little thing, but the lives that my mother destroyed over that affair, along with her subsequent related lies were horrible!

Page 15, paragraph 2 says: *"I could not collect child support from Ed* (my father) *because he was classified by the V. A. as "mentally disabled". Lynn* (Menard) *just refused to pay anything. Neither father ever visited their children, all their growing up years. They never sent so much as a ten cent toy at Christmas or on birthdays."*

Two more bald-faced lies! My father's PARTIAL disability pension was so small that the court ordered him to pay $15.00 per month for child support for three kids. That wouldn't have bought bird feed for a couple of parakeets for a month! Mama didn't even try to get that small pocket change but why would she—it would have done nothing! Daddy did refuse to try to work. He was mentally and emotionally challenged so maybe he couldn't, I don't know!

As a result of Mama's personal choice, manipulation, and actions, Menard had no idea where his kids were for at least two years after we arrived in California. He COULDN'T have paid child support!

Menard FINALLY found out where we were because Mama went on Welfare while pregnant with April. When she signed up for Welfare she was forced to give them the father's names of the baby and her other children. The D. A.'s office went after Menard for child support. He was, by then, working for the sanitation company in Austin, Texas. In order to keep his job he HAD to pay child support, and did, DIRECTLY TO Mama. She cashed the checks every month and LIED to the Welfare Department, the two kids AND her relatives, stating Menard wouldn't pay. When the Welfare Department caught her she was scared and admitted to me that they had filed a fraud charge against her. She almost went to jail for Welfare Fraud. She immediately had her welfare checks reduced for a long time in order to pay back the excess money they'd allotted to her!

After that Menard's checks went directly to the Welfare Department until his two kids turned eighteen! (She drew welfare from her pregnancy with April until she got the job with the men's prison.) But Mama had already done maximum damage to those kids by constantly telling them their daddy didn't care anything about them and wouldn't help with child support.

Margie says Menard and his new wife began sending presents to Paw Paw and Mama Davis' house for the kids when they were still very small but Mama would open them and then throw the gifts away without telling the kids! She lied about EVERYTHING!

Menard and his wife did visit the kids when they were teenagers but by then it was too late. He was a stranger and they'd been taught to hate him.

My father didn't have the money or the wish to travel all the way to California—he would have had to do it on the bus, and then where would he have stayed? He couldn't stay at my mother's or my grandparents! Yet Mama did send the two boys back to live with him when Frankie was about eleven. They stayed for a year and were miserable. So was Daddy.

Page 19, paragraph 7: in regard to her hijacking/kidnapping us to Fresno, California: *". . . packed our few clothes and with my children migrated to Fresno . . . the transition was hard for Laura* (Me!) *The children and I had no time to be a family unit"!*

***MIGRATED*?!** There was no "migration"! There was a bunch of her lies, manipulation, huge broken promises, and stolen property!

"No time to be a family unit"?! Mama had NEVER been interested in her kids OR anything relating to "family"! All she wanted was a MAN!!

Last but not least: Page 20, paragraph 7:   *"I'm not going to give Satan any glory by going into detail about my life that I spent in a backslidden condition, other than what I have related here. I never meant to defy my Lord or to break His Commandments."*

Very convenient! Invent a fairy tale life, steal incidents from other's lives and pretend they're yours, make up stories about how spiritual you are and then refuse to *"give Satan the glory"* by telling anything you might have done wrong! Trouble was she continued her normal, usual behavior until the end of her life!

Yes, all people sin, all people make mistakes! I've made many. But if you're really serious you not only repent, you GO THE OTHER WAY! You don't KEEP committing the same behaviors over and over claiming to be such a devout Christian!

Oh, there are lots more imaginations and out-right lies in her "book". However, there were a few things in her "book" that anyone in the world—if they were thinking as they read—would catch: On page eleven, for example:

"When I was nineteen, I met the young man that I would eventually marry. It was early in the year of 1947. We met at church. The bloody conflagration that we refer to as World War II had recently ended. He was just out of the army. He was five feet seven, sandy haired and always neatly dressed. He was quiet and soft spoken. Everyone seemed to like him. We would go, after church to a nearby restaurant that was popular with the young crowd. We would sit and talk and listen to the juke box. Elvis Presley was the big thing on the juke box back then."

All of that is a flat out fairy tale! My birthday per my formal Texas birth certificate is Sept. 2, 1947. She and Daddy were married, per the official Texas copy of their marriage certificate that I obtained in the early '80's while doing genealogy research, on June 15, 1946. She even says on page 13 that *"Fifteen months after we* (she and my father) *were married, I gave birth to a beautiful blonde haired baby girl"* (which would be ME!) However, the wrong dates are the least important parts of this lie.

The next point to get out of the way is: neither my mother nor my father ever danced in their entire lives and they would not have gone to a teenage hangout filled with people! Daddy was extremely uncomfortable in groups (I believe he had at least a touch of agoraphobia) and he never learned any social skills. He would never have gone to a crowded place to "sit and talk". He would never even eat inside a restaurant, primarily because he was so cheap but the few times he bought cheap burgers (five or six for a dollar) he'd always get them to go and we'd have to eat them in his car no matter how hot or cold it was outdoors. He especially would not have gotten up in front of people and tried to dance.

Neither would my mother! She wouldn't even try to learn to do things like play cards or any other games or sports so that she and her boyfriends could socialize with others—all she did was work, go to school, or stay home—she would NOT socialize! The night I turned 21 Mama insisted on accompanying me and my best friend to celebrate my birthday. We went to a popular country night club by the name, "Nashville West" in Fresno, where I tried to get Mama to dance (she was asked a couple of times) but she refused saying she'd never learned to dance and couldn't! She was always afraid of looking silly or out of control in front of others.

But the HUGE LIE HERE is: Elvis was born January 8, 1935. He would have been eleven years old in 1946!! He didn't hit the stage until circa 1956 or '57. They couldn't have sat and listened to him on the jukebox!

One of her sisters caught this blatant lie about Elvis and challenged her on it. Mama argued and argued, "No! It's TRUE, I remember it well!" until that sister proved to her Elvis' birthday.

Then all of a sudden Mama backed down, said, "Oh, I guess you're right. I'll have to change that before I publish it!"

She was my mother and I kept hoping she'd change. I tried to forgive her for the things she continued to do to us. But she was a pathological-lying, mentally/emotionally ill human being to the very end!

I always knew what she was just from her actions over the years. I didn't need the following admission in her "book", which just MAY be the only truth in the entire manuscript! (However, we can't know for sure. This could be a fabrication as well to try to make herself look more of a victim.)

She relates on page 8 the following about her fourteenth year: *"I began to exhibit weird symptoms that I could neither control nor understand. Unexpected periods of numbness would come over me, especially in my face. My head would ache, I would get dizzy and my vision would become fuzzy. Everything around me would fade into a kind of grey mist, sounds around me seemed to come from a distance and everything around me would seem alien and strange. I would try to speak and my speech would come out in unintelligible sounds that were just silly, garbled nonsense. I thought it was funny and I would laugh. Mother* (Mama Davis) *would yell at me to stop my foolishness. These episodes happened quite frequently for sometime but I finally got over it. Once more I praised the Lord for delivering me from what I now believe was a mental breakdown."*

I happen to believe these "episodes" could have been schizophrenic breaks or something similar! She was one sick human being her entire life! I think if she had gotten help she could have lived a better, more normal life. I know for sure her children, grandchildren, and co-workers (who all, at one point or another, would find themselves on the receiving end of her rages and lies) would have been much better off! But she refused.

Mama couldn't admit any of her bad behavior and she always tried to smear anyone who brought to light her misdeeds. My dad tried to tell me that many times when I was young but I didn't believe him. He'd say, "She only wants people to like her!"

By 2002 when I wrote my first book I had become fully aware of that. But I didn't change the names of characters, or novelize *Time & Again* because I wanted to hide her identity. I did it because I was hiding MINE!! I didn't want to admit to the world that was my story! I didn't expose her! It was she that told everybody I was writing horrible lies about her in my book!

I kept her "book" and sent her a letter to let her know her I had a copy and it wasn't going to work. I was blunt. She'd written that she intended to submit her "book" to churches to try to help others find their way out of horrible lives just like she had by prayer, living by the Bible, etc. I let her know I would NOT allow lies like those spread throughout her book to go unchallenged, and as a California State Licensed Fraud Investigator for at least fifteen years by that time; she knew I had the wherewithal to do it! I reminded her there are records and eye witnesses to almost everything in the most unusual places and I knew how to get my hands on them! I heard no more about "publishing".

Then she went into Projection mode. Projection is a psychological term that means a person denies the existence of unconscious impulses or qualities in themselves while attributing those same qualities to others. She started the rumor that I was claiming to be a Christian and yet was currently involved in a TORRID love affair with a married man in my church! The relatives grabbed and ran with that one! Since a man any man—was Mama's focus all her life she apparently was under the assumption that all women felt the same.

However, the people who knew me, including my two grown children of whom I've always had a very close relationship, knew I hadn't been on a SINGLE DATE in thirteen years!

At that time my daughter still lived at home and had been trying for years to get me to start dating. I refused. I'd tease her and tell her I had five absolute characteristics ANY MAN I considered would have to have and of course those five things were just about impossible to find in one human being. The least important of those characteristics was that the guy had to be an experienced guitar player so he could back up my five string banjo playing! (Yes, I had gotten much deeper into music.) That drove my daughter to distraction.

However, the real reason I wouldn't attempt another relationship was because I'd been married twice, both husbands had been bad choices—one an extremely emotionally distant man, and the other a rabid, pathological liar. Wonder where I picked up the subconscious urge to pick partners who exhibited those two characteristics?! I'd decided in the eighties that I would not be like my mother and keep picking unhealthy partners—I was going to learn what my problems were and how to heal them. I wouldn't date again until I had accomplished that!

The only thing Mama's "book" and lies about my life did was cause more hostility between her children and relatives that were still living. And believe me she'd caused a lot of that before either of our books! She just couldn't stand that any of us might get along with each other so she stirred up lies and rumors behind our backs and none of us realized it for many years. Several still believe everything she said—but I can't hold it against them. I was well into my forth decade before I realized the totality of her toxicity and decided to separate myself from it. No matter how old you get you still want your Mama! But I finally realized, once and for all, I had never had a mother!

I also learned several new things Mama had said behind my back years before: when I graduated from college in 1976, and was awarded the magna cum laude honors, she told her family (Margie was one) that the only reason I did that was "because I wanted to show her up". Remember, she'd graduated cum laude—I graduated with the next highest honors; magna cum laude. That revelation depressed me all over again. I had been so proud of what she'd done in school and I was trying to follow that example; just doing the best I could!

Before my book I had forgiven Mama by faith because I knew she had problems. I'd stopped believing anything she said many years before. I prayed often that someday we could put aside the ugliness and heal our relationship. But I can tell you the lengths she went to try to destroy me because of my book, *Time & Again*, caused me to have a horrific time sticking to my determination to forgive her. I decided to write "the rest of the story"!

In 2005 I published the sequel to *Time & Again*. The title of that one was *Time Will Tell*. I still wasn't ready to announce to the world what I'd lived through. I kept the fake names for the characters but again I told the truth about our "family" in California. I am finally okay with people knowing what we went through. I've also been at peace for many years.

Mama didn't like my second book either!

Several years after her rebuttal "book" when she knew her end was near (2008) she called me up and started berating me over the "lies" Margie and I had told about her. I tried to talk to her but she kept yelling so I finally said gently, "I'm not doing this. Rest in peace."

I hung up and cried off and on for several days, not because I still wanted her love or approval but because neither I, nor my siblings had ever had it! It was such a waste of life! Theoretically AND literally! I had two brothers who'd died, Frankie and Terry Lee and I've always believed the lack of love and family, and the neglect and abuse, contributed mightily to both deaths! I know what it did to the rest of us who are still living!

During my brother, Terry's last days he called me and asked, "Linda, if we were so poor we couldn't afford enough food for all of us, why was Mama always so fat?" (She was probably fifty or sixty pounds overweight most of Terry's life.) He, Karen, and April were skinny little kids. And so were Frankie, Gary and I when we were growing up. It was obvious Terry was "reliving" parts of his life, searching for answers. I knew she ate away from home but it wouldn't do Terry any good to tell him that—he wanted a caring mother as well. I just said, "Well, our foods were mostly starches, Terry."

Mama died a couple of weeks after her last phone call to me. I didn't go to her funeral service but my son who is a Pastor officiated at it. I provided photographs of her at different ages for the video. I didn't go because of the blatant hostility of my two younger half-sisters and a couple of other hostile relatives who were going to be there. I knew if I showed up there'd be some ugly stuff go down. I chose peace, instead. Besides, if you can't get along in person, why go to a funeral and pretend?

Did I hate my mother? No!

Did I love her? I loved the person I always hoped she'd "grow" into. After so many years and so many betrayals, No I didn't love her—something inside her was very broken! I don't believe you can continue to love someone you can't trust and respect. I did continue to pray for her.

Did I miss her after she died? No. I was sad a few days because the chance to heal our relationship would never happen, but mostly I felt relief. She couldn't hurt any of us anymore.

Chapter Thirteen

I was wrong about only having one book in me, though. This is my seventh and it just may be the most important one—planned specifically to pay tribute to those wonderful, average people from Everman Drive who had supersized hearts. They took me in, supported me, taught me valuable lessons, and yes, I think, at least some of them even loved me a little bit! I have forged a great life, mostly because of God and the people of Everman Drive.

There are no words to adequately thank and show them my appreciation for what they did for me. A lot of them have passed on—especially those I was closest to, so it's way too late to tell them, although I did include a few in my second book, *Time Will Tell*. Others may not remember me I was there such a short time.

When I found my friend Linda Drinning in approximately 2009, one of my main goals was to find Mary and Harry Lee to let them know what they'd meant to me. My next goal was to have Linda take me to Everman Drive once more when I visited Dallas in 2010.

I was very sad when she informed me that Mary and Harry Lee's marriage hadn't made it past the seventies and that they'd lost their son Sidney—they had three sons total. Harry Lee had eventually married again and had two daughters. I believe Mary had also remarried. I'm not sure if she had more children but I do know she became a beautician and owned her own shop.

The most difficult thing to hear was that Harry Lee passed away in 1985. He was forty-three years old. Linda said the church where his funeral was held was packed to capacity with friends, neighbors, and co-employees. The church was so full that day there were many, many people who had to stand outside. That doesn't surprise me!

Linda also told me of others who'd passed: Mr. and Mrs. Drinning quite some time ago, Linda's sister Dellie in 2001, her brothers Gerald and Danny in 2013, Margaret Rose Springer, Brenda Burkett, William and Charlene Stockton, and D.C. Cantrell. J. W. Springer, who'd married Charlene Stockton, was said at that time to be in a fight for his life with a terminal disease. He has since passed away.

I did get to see and visit with Linda's sister Nelda on my trip to Texas in 2010 and yes, we reminisced a little bit about old Ace the horse that she and I both loved. Nelda passed away in 2014.

Another heartbreaking revelation was that I'd never see Everman Drive again. It had been demolished in about 1977. The houses were either torn down or moved away, the residents relocated to other areas. The entire neighborhood had been turned into a fenced and locked city or county yard of some sort. Talk about disappointment!

After the neighborhood was demolished there were several organized resident reunions scattered over several years. I didn't know about them and probably wouldn't have been able to go even if I had. But the reunions prove I wasn't the only one who knew that place, those people, and that time were very, very special!

But Linda and her husband Johnny did take me by Linfield Elementary School which had been locked up and used for storage for many years. I took pictures—that old tether ball pole was still standing—and then I went home and grieved. I still grieve from time to time. It's all gone.

Menard died not too long after his visit to see his two children in California.

Daddy died in 1998.

Frankie died of a massive heart attack in about 1999. I'd been estranged from Frankie for many, many years but I heard that drugs and alcohol that he'd started in his early teen years had taken a toll on his health and heart and contributed greatly to his early death.

Gary became embroiled in his own problems and battles, some he won, some he didn't. Unfortunately he and I have had no contact in over twenty years.

Terry Lee survived his awful childhood, found Jesus and a wonderful Christian wife, fathered three sweet girls and then succumbed in his late-thirties, in the early 2000's, to a devastating blood disease. Mama had caused a rift in mine and Terry's relationship when he was in his early teens by telling him lies about me and telling me lies about him. We were estranged until a couple of years before his death. I'm so grateful that God got us together and we were able to talk and straighten out the crooked paths of our lives before he passed.

I've had no personal contact in twenty or thirty years with Karen or April outside of running into April in a bathroom of a church once for a few minutes years ago,—it's hard to keep track of the time. Both of them have had big problems.

Linda's husband, Johnny Van Briggle passed away in 2014.

It's not easy to turn one's life around! I discovered I had to let people—mostly my family members—go. I had to strengthen my spine, gather my determination, throw my shoulders back, grit my teeth and go to work on myself—no excuses!

And . . . I had to find Jesus! I began that search in my mid-thirties but didn't get serious about it and start "walking the walk" until my forties. I'm still not perfect and still working on becoming the person I aspire to be but I am so much better than I used to be! The credit goes to God. He healed me of a decades-long battle with crippling, severe panic-anxiety syndrome which was leading into agoraphobia in the nineties. The fear, worry, uncertainty, shaming, isolation, etc. of the first half of my life took a heavy toll. But, I haven't had even one panic attack since 1995! Praise God!

I made lots of mega-bad, wrong, and even stupid decisions in my life. I made some terrible choices. I wasn't proud of them then, and I'm not now. I hurt a lot of people even though I tried not to. I've apologized and asked forgiveness from those I can find.

One of those I hurt the most was ME! I wish I had known my worth! I grew up accepting second and third best in everything and continued that even after I graduated from college. But success does lead to more success. You have to stick your neck out and take chances if you want to succeed. Success causes you to gain confidence. Confidence causes you to step out and try for more! I'm so glad I learned that!

But one of the things I'm most proud of is I was able to break the generational curse that dogged both sides of my family for generations!

My two kids (adults on their own for years now) knew growing up and know now, they are LOVED! I made mistakes but we all do no matter how hard we try.

Both my kids are artists in different mediums and have made good money doing it.

My son—my first born—obtained his B. A. in psychology, his Masters in Divinity, and his Doctorate in Ministry. He is a Pastor and an author of six wonderful, inspirational books. He travels internationally teaching the Word of God.

My daughter is absolutely beautiful inside and out, and works in the medical field. I am amazed at how many dozens of wonderful, loyal friends she has. Everybody loves her! But she's a little spit fire as well—nobody walks on my baby! Her secret is that she's a great friend herself—she adheres to the old saying: "if you want friends you have to be a friend!" She's got a ton of them!

It took many years—half my life AND GOD—to create the kind of character and life that I always knew in the core of my being that I could have. I'm proud of my accomplishments and my blessings but I won't quit now. I've done my best to give others "a hand up" and will continue to do that, as well as keep trying to improve myself!

A huge helping of gratitude goes to my Everman Drive friends. They provided the pattern. I will never forget them.

I believe beyond a shadow of a doubt that Harry Lee and Mary would be proud of me today. They never had a clue how much they meant to me.

I tried to tell Mary in the only phone call I was able to have with her in 2009 but I don't think she understood or completely accepted the depth of my gratitude. Of course, she did say she had been working in her beauty shop for several days, long hours, without a day off, and that she was exhausted, but it also had been so many years she may not have retained the same level of memories that I have. (I had to smile when she told me about her beauty shop—I just may have been her first model!)

And, I know beyond a shadow of a doubt that I'll see Harry Lee again someday. He'll be one of the first coming to greet me. We may not have memories in heaven of Everman Drive but I'll know my earthly "big brother" when I see him, and boy does he have a big hug coming! Then he and the rest of my loved ones will turn to our REAL "big Brother" Jesus, and He'll show us what love and hugs really are!

Made in the USA
Middletown, DE
20 July 2022